The University in a Developing World Society

ONE HUNDRED AND TWENTY-FIFTH
ANNIVERSARY CELEBRATION
1842–1967

THE UNIVERSITY IN A DEVELOPING WORLD SOCIETY

A Commemorative Volume

Presented by
THE UNIVERSITY OF NOTRE DAME

Copyright ©
1968
University of Notre Dame
Notre Dame, Indiana

Library of Congress Card No. 68-25118

PREFACE

WHAT A WORLD SOCIETY MIGHT NECESSITATE AND even what it might be like were by no means new ideas even at the time of the founding of the University of Notre Dame in 1842 in the State of Indiana in the United States of America. Although there had not as yet been any world wars and although the world was then a much larger place, some of it still unexplored, the vision of a world order, a true international community of man, was not at all unknown. The fact that the University of Notre Dame was founded by a French priest, a member of the Congregation of Holy Cross, was in itself some indication that representatives of individual nations wanted to share in a larger, common and more noble destiny.

Whether Father Sorin, at the time he established this university, saw it as one of the great means for furthering and forwarding the idea of the world society which would eventually come into being is not completely clear. He may well have had some presage of this sort. Again, the historical fact is that he established a university, knowing full well that, at least in the beginning, his university would be a rather pale reflection of some of the great universities of his native land and of other European countries. Whatever else midwestern America needed, it certainly needed the power and civilizing influence of education.

When Notre Dame reached its one hundredth anniversary in 1942, the second of the World Wars was in progress and only a very limited observance was possible.

The Committee which planned this Symposium in connection with the celebration of Notre Dame's one hundred and twenty-fifth anniversary felt that in the years since its founding, Notre Dame had emerged as a university of some international and even worldwide prominence. In this Notre Dame joined hands with many of its sister universities throughout the land and around the world. The Committee felt, further, that it would be both exciting and significant to explore how the university as such, surely one of the institutions of major importance in the world of today, understood and faced its responsibilities toward the world society which, though still developing and uncertain and insecure, is now more necessary than ever. The basic assumption is that the universities, more than any other institution in society, will shape the ways in which the human beings of the world learn to live together— or die together—on this or other planets.

There are four papers in this academic symposium, each dealing with a certain aspect of the university's role in a developing world society. Clearly the subject is a momentous one as befits the occasion. There could have been other papers included and each of the authors might have approached his

Preface

subject from another and different point of view. But the symposium was intended to introduce the subject, not at all to exhaust it. It draws its fundamental unity from the fact that each of the authors considers what the university is and should be as it faces a future in which the survival of mankind may well depend on whether it is possible to develop a viable world society, in spirit as well as in form and structure.

Father Reinert discusses the responsibilities and opportunities of the university as they pertain to the inmost life of man, i.e., his spiritual and religious aspirations. Dr. Sanford in speaking of the university and the life of the student emphasizes that in time we will come to see that "our own humanity and that of other people must be realized together." Dr. DuBridge explains that the university, as fountainhead of knowledge, contributes to the developing of a world society precisely because it is a center of teaching and learning, a center of scholarship and research. Father Hesburgh, the fifteenth President of the University of Notre Dame, speaking at the Special Academic Convocation commemorating the one hundred and twenty-fifth anniversary of the founding of the University, charts the course for the building of a great modern Catholic university and indicates how such a university might best participate in the developing of a world society by moving every scholar within the university to look beyond his immediate field of vision to the total landscape of God and man and the universe.

John E. Walsh, C.S.C.

The reader will notice several subthemes running through the symposium papers: that the university must be free and autonomous; that it should stress values as well as ideas; that the best universities are those in which the professors are genuinely interested in students at the same time they are deeply dedicated to scholarship and research; that the university is directly concerned with man's humanity, his dignity, his welfare and his progress everywhere; in short, that society, now and in the future, will reflect the quality and purpose and leadership of the universities.

Since this is a commemorative volume, it includes, in addition to the symposium, the homily delivered at the Anniversary Mass by His Excellency, Most Reverend Luigi Raimondi, Apostolic Delegate to the United States; a statement by Mr. Edmund Stephen, of Chicago, Chairman of the Board of Trustees; greetings to the University of Notre Dame from Pope Paul VI and from Lyndon B. Johnson, President of the United States.

As Chairman of the Anniversary Celebration Committee, I would like to express the gratitude of the University of Notre Dame to all those who came from some one hundred colleges and universities to celebrate with us. Our special thanks to those who shared their ideas with us and to those here on the campus who worked so diligently to make our celebration both a proper and a memorable one.

CONTENTS

PREFACE
Reverend John E. Walsh, C.S.C.
Vice President, Academic Affairs

THE UNIVERSITY AND THE INMOST
LIFE OF MAN   1
Reverend Paul C. Reinert, S.J.
President, Saint Louis University

THE UNIVERSITY: FOUNTAINHEAD
OF KNOWLEDGE   25
Dr. Lee A. DuBridge
President, California Institute of Technology

THE UNIVERSITY AND THE LIFE OF THE
STUDENT: THE NEXT 100 YEARS   43
Dr. Nevitt Sanford
Professor of Psychology and Education
Director, Institute for the Study of Human Problems at Stanford

THE VISION OF A GREAT CATHOLIC
UNIVERSITY IN THE WORLD TODAY   63
Reverend Theodore M. Hesburgh, C.S.C.
President, University of Notre Dame

SERMON 87
   Most Reverend Luigi Raimondi
   Apostolic Delegate to the United States

REMARKS 97
   Mr. Edmund A. Stephan
   Chairman, Board of Trustees, University of Notre Dame

LETTERS FROM: 102
   Pope Paul VI
   President Lyndon B. Johnson

THE UNIVERSITY AND
THE INMOST LIFE OF MAN

Paul C. Reinert, S. J.

AT THIS CELEBRATION OF THE HUNDRED AND twenty-fifth anniversary of the founding of Notre Dame there could hardly be a more appropriate theme than the one which has been chosen: "The University in a Developing World Society," for Notre Dame can look back to her past role in such development with a pride exceeded only by the confidence in the role which the future will give to her.

The theme itself is so comprehensive, however, and the responsibilities of a university so multiple now and in the future that one can hardly hope to deal with them in their entirety. Three such responsibilities have been singled out for discussion in this academic symposium, and so before turning to an extended treatment of my particular subject, the responsibility of the university to what I shall call the inmost life of man, I would like briefly to situate it in relationship to those other two facets of this total responsibility.

Paul C. Reinert, S.J.

First, it is almost a cliché to say that we are all inextricably involved in the turmoil and the promise of a developing world society. Of course, a cliché is such in part because it is so obviously true. Such a society has come into being and is in the process of development in large measure because of an almost exponential extension and refinement of knowledge over the past few centuries. To see how true this is in an academic context, we have only to look at the research journals ranged over ever-increasing lengths of library shelves, or we need only count the scholarly publications too numerous in any one field to be dealt with other than in *Abstracts,* which themselves threaten to engulf the serious student. Knowing we shall fail, we can only try to keep up with the neverending round of conventions, congresses and conferences, devoted to serious consideration of any one or more of hundreds of scholarly fields. And such progression gives little or no sign of any abatement in the future other than in the utter madness of an atomic holocaust carried out by powers which have most benefited from this knowledge explosion. To this extension and refinement of knowledge as a key element in a developing world society the university quite rightly addresses itself, and it takes on a responsibility commensurate with its high calling.

Yet, the university takes on such a responsibility in a particular context different from that of a pure research institute or a technical governmental bureau. It is the context of a community, a shared

The University and the Inmost Life of Man

community of scholars and students, engaged ideally, however far short we fall in practice, in a common interactive venture. To some of the implication of community I shall come later in this paper. For the moment, and for every moment in the life of the university, it is important to recall that if this is indeed such a community of persons, then the university has to be concerned, beyond simple knowledge, with the personal needs of its members, and especially of its students as they engage in their last formal preparation for mature roles in such a rapidly changing society as ours is. This, the specific responsibility to the needs of its students, is the second area of discussion in the present symposium.

Neither the expansion and refinement of knowledge nor the personal needs of the newer members of the academic community are situated in a vacuum. They do not exist in a solipsistic or even a privatistic world. They are ineluctably situated within the context of a world of political and social forms. Though these forms are not an immediate concern of this symposium, they are concurrently shaped by ourselves while they in turn shape us. For our own sakes and for a future developing world society, the university must be concerned with a critical appraisal of and an imaginative program for such forms and institutions. It must concern itself with the knowledge and intelligent compassion which its students will, as fully participating citizens, bring to their shaping of the political and social institutions of tomorrow. The university cannot help being, directly and indirectly, a major social institution, and as such it will have, say yea or say no, an influence on the politics of our world.

It is in the context of these university engagements in a developing world that I now turn to what may be, perhaps, an even more fundamental responsibility of the university, and one even more difficult of fulfillment: What is the responsibility of the university to the inmost life of man?

Let me describe rather than define what is meant by this term, the inmost life of man. When we have concerned ourselves as deeply as possible with the expansion of knowledge, with the needs of the students, and with the political and social order of the future, when we have implemented those concerns to the best of our ability, an ultimate "why?" still remains. This "why" sums up, all too poignantly at times, the need felt by every society, every age, every culture, and by every man for answers to ultimate questions. To the problem of the university's involvement in such questions I wish to address myself. This is the problem of how the university copes with, comes to terms with, engages itself in a facet of reality with which it seems regularly to have found itself acutely uncomfortable.

Like it or not, praise it or decry it, the university cannot ignore or wish away the fact that man does ask ultimate questions, does have metaphysical problems, does structure his most basic anxieties and his most radical hopes, his deepest sorrows and his almost inexpressible joys into meaningful systems of belief and practice, whether these beliefs and practices be specifically religious or not. Does the university have any obligation to assist man in this neverending search for an overarching principle of unity, for the nature of transcendence, for the ultimate purpose of being, for the root source of the total "otherness" which he all too often experiences? Should the university enter into the area of the images and symbols and values by which man has always sought to express and cope with his deepest interior experiences?

My answer to this most serious of questions is that the university has no choice but to do so. The university in this presently developing world society *does* have a responsibility to assist man in his stirring toward those spiritual, religious, metaphysical, ultimate, call them what you will, ideals and aspirations. They are not only man's most intimate glory and most intimate cross, they also play so significant a role in giving richness and power and depth to all the facets of what we call the processes of civilization and culture.

I know, of course, that in more recent times the university has been highly reluctant to venture outside the realm of almost purely intellectual development as its overridingly primary task. And I—as all of us—must respect this single-minded concern, born out of an utterly sincere desire to develop the mind of modern man to its fullest, a fullness which always exceeds our ability to provide for it. Yet, I repeat that this is now not enough. It is increasingly borne in upon the thoughtful observer that for all the expansion of knowledge, for all the concern for the immediate material wants of man, for all the hopes put in the perfecting of a just political and social system, there is still an ever-growing feeling that present day man is cut adrift, without ultimate meaning and without guiding purpose for his life.

I maintain that this drift will continue unless the university enters into the situation. More importantly, I maintain that in many instances only the university can do something about it. The university is the only modern instrumentality which will be able to cope with this malaise of emptiness, this seemingly hollow and vacuous reecho of the question "Why?".

These are startling statements, I know, and perhaps I ought briefly to make clear what, in playing such a role, the university is and is *not*. I am not suggesting that the university is or should be a surrogate church, nor do I at all think that knowledge is a substitute for religious faith. Nor is the university to be a substitute Maecenas, providing redemption or at least ultimate meaning through the higher forms of artistic endeavor. I am simply saying that there is no other institution realistically available to many men to help them effectively in this most basic of queries. Not the family, nor the state, nor any economic organization, nor any ideology, not even the church in the sense of any particular religious body. Whether any one of the foregoing ought to be available, whether any one of them is in itself

The University and the Inmost Life of Man

a better instrumentality, whether man ought to choose one of them, is not the question here and now. Here and now, it seems to me, only the university can begin—and I say *begin* advisedly—can begin to fill this void.

Why is this so? As over the last several centuries, little by little, man's view of nature and man's view of his own nature have changed; as man became "modern man," he has been emancipating himself, albeit often unknowingly, from his ancient signposts and anchor holds of custom and tradition. Much of the western world lives today amid the personal consequences of emancipation from established authority, and if we are to believe the signs of the times, such a Western world is to be the paradigm for other lands and other peoples. In the course of this emancipation and in the course of the rationalization of so much of our lives, the old signposts of a fixed and traditional order, the comforting, or at least solid, authority of unchanging ecclesiastical or political orders, the cake of custom, the support of discipline, the surety of social status, the certainty of usage, all have progressively been left behind.

The guides to which a man could turn in his questioning have so often lost existence or, perhaps more often, credibility. But the questions remain. What is good? What is true? Who am I? What am I doing here? Why am I at all? And the questions are often an oblique way of affirming that there is a mystery about the human person and his destiny, that there is something about our being here which is unsettled and unfinished.

If such is the nature of man (if one may be permitted to use that somewhat unfashionable phrase), or if such is at any rate his existential condition, if he continues to ask such questions, why should it be the university to which he turns, indeed in many cases, must turn for an answer? First, so many of the other repositories of what man has believed to be true have either abdicated their authority or lost their credibility. Second, rightly or wrongly, the university, the company of scholars, has so remade man's vision of the world and of himself, has answered so many questions, that in modern man's mind it is now burdened with the task and credited with the ability to provide answers to yet further questions and to remake man's vision of his interior world, of his interior self.

He has no other place to go. He has the university community alone now to fall back upon. Most importantly, he still has his ultimate questions.

It is on this ineluctable questioning proper to and inherent in every man that the university's responsibility to the inmost life of man is founded. As I have briefly suggested, the nature of such a responsibility is not to be confused with that of church or state or family or any other social organ. It is of a nature appropriate to the nature of the university itself, and so must involve intelligence, knowledge, wisdom, in a community of persons.

How such a responsibility ought in general to

The University and the Inmost Life of Man

function I would here like to investigate with you. Obviously, we must begin with the primary concerns of a university: intelligence, knowledge, wisdom. First, and most evidently, the university must take with utmost seriousness its task of the general expansion of knowledge. All knowledge, directly or indirectly, helps ultimately to get at the interior of man. Furthermore, I would say personally as a Christian that such a duty is even more incumbent upon the Christian personally and upon the university which calls itself Christian. Why? Simply from the general logic of the Incarnation, it seems to me. The Christian is committed to this world and to the deepest understanding of it possible, for all the reasons that anyone else can urge, from the alleviation of physical evil to the increase in purely speculative knowledge, simply because knowledge is eminently good in itself. But beyond that, for a Christian, man and the world take on even further significance. This world is not only valuable in itself, but it is *trans*valued by God becoming incarnate in it in Christ. Not only is man the highest of human goods and a value unto himself, but since God became man in Christ, man is now a value even *beyond* himself. We might ask how seriously the university community has taken the expansion of knowledge, even on the most basic level, and to the painful point of resolutely putting in a subordinate position *all* that does not first and foremost so contribute.

Secondly, and yet more specifically, it seems to me

that the university can fulfill responsibility to the inmost life of man by giving in the future much more attention, much more time, and much more money and prestige to those disciplines which the more directly deal with man. Please do not misunderstand: I am not suggesting that the university close down its physics facilities or decide to do no more mathematical research, or stop its involvement in geology or any other such discipline. But I am saying that since our resources are not unlimited and since not all things can be done to an equal degree, it may well be that the university might better turn far more attention than in the past to such fields as deal with man in community and man in singularity. If we take as seriously as we ought the ultimate questions that man asks, should we not find out more about man himself, in psychology, in sociology, in genetics, in cultural anthropology, in economics, in philosophy, in political science, and in history? Perhaps, and it is only a perhaps, the university can best serve man by more concentration of resources herein than it has given to such studies in the past.

To go further, when we have to choose (and I wish we did not have to), between a new electron microscope and an acquisition for our art gallery, between a campus computer and a campus fountain, do we hesitate long enough to include in our decisions the factors that make for man being more deeply man in the presence of beauty?

But all of this, valuable as it might be, is still

The University and the Inmost Life of Man

essentially peripheral to the intellectual discipline which deals with the inmost life of man as it engages itself in relation to that which is both closest to that inmost life and which at the same time is utterly beyond it, God. I mean, of course, theology, in its widest meanings and in all its varied parts. To recall for a moment what I mean by this "inmost life," we need only recall that we do ask ourselves "What is the universe *doing?*" If all reality is a happening, what is happening, what is going on? What does the very presence of life tell me, and especially what is conscious life all about? Where did this "I" come from, this "I" that no one else can say, this "I" which is just that personal and equally fragile, and yet upon which for me all the rest depends? What difference does it make what I do, and why do I want others to approve of what I do? Finally, what possible reason or meaning does death, the extinction of this personal "I," contain? We ask these questions now. Man has always asked them. Because they get at the inner heart of man, we have no reason to believe he will not continue to ask them, century upon century.

I do not suggest that of itself theology, or even the busy and arduous study of it, will yield the final answers satisfying to this "I" that is myself. Why this is so I shall speak of in a few moments. But I do affirm that this subject can and does address itself directly to the questions, that it can and does have something ordered and coherent and intelligent to say about man and his situation, and that pursued in conjunction especially with the other disciplines that treat of man, it can and does illuminate the human condition.

To do so, however, such studies must be undertaken and carried on at the same level of scholarly competence, rigor, devotion and humility as are other university fields. It would seem to follow then that if the university is going to be true to the existential situation of man, it will have to take such studies seriously and sympathetically. On the other hand, if theology is seriously to help meet—not to meet, but to *help meet*—man's inmost needs in a world society in which knowledge is becoming increasingly complicated, sophisticated and interrelated, I do not see how it can begin to do so except in the context wherein these attributes of knowledge have been most seriously developed and investigated, that is, within a university context.

Theology must be researched, studied, developed, criticized, transmitted, within the vital milieu of the modern university. We can only rejoice at the recent and planned integrations and reintegrations of theological faculties into total university communities, and at the increasing support given to such studies by universities fortunate enough already to have them. We must also hope that other universities will experience their incompleteness without such studies.

But much more remains to be done. Among the most important tasks are two which have far-ranging implications. First, the university must exert every effort to initiate and encourage interdisciplinary

The University and the Inmost Life of Man

studies of the sort that will bring ultimate questions into confrontation with more proximate problems and findings. Full many an overarching theory can fall under the accumulated weight of humble empirical evidence to the contrary. More than one theological proposition may be better off—and the men who hold that it illuminates man's condition better off, too—if it and they enter into relation with other truths which throws a far different light on that same condition. The more they who seek to structure and order possibly ultimate answers enter into commerce with those who look for the structure and order of man and the world here and now, the better off both may be. It does not mean that wholehearted acceptance of each other's insights will follow. But at least each may become increasingly aware of the complexity of man and the difficulty of communication across the gulfs that separate not only different structures of knowledge but the men themselves who often so genuinely want to communicate. We are often dimly aware of asking the same questions, even if we find so desperately that we are not speaking the same language in asking them.

If this is true of interdisciplinary studies in which the theological disciplines are to play a serious part, it is perhaps even more necessary that the university put its prestige and its resources behind what might be called interideological studies. By this I mean teaching and research not only in such subjects as the philosophy of religion or the sociology of belief or the history of theology, but also comparative religious studies, and comparative value system studies, not at all excluding but rather welcoming specifically nontheistic systems such as ethical humanism. Surely the religiously committed universities of this country should be beyond the stage where they think they have nothing to gain from the men who seriously attempt to confront the human dilemma on the purely human level. Sometimes the poignant realization by such scholars that this is the only level to which they hold can give added intensity to their search. Likewise, one can hope that the "secular," religiously "noncommitted" university recognizes or is coming to the recognition that noncommitment is in itself a philosophical stance open to serious investigation. In addition, the calm and reasoned commitment to a faith or vision of life on the part of many unambiguously qualified members of the academic community argues for an attempt to treat such commitments sympathetically, and to take them seriously in a continuing scholarly investigation of the values we live by, values which are often religious.

Perhaps most importantly, the university community of the western world will have to open itself much more not only to its own western religious and ethical heritages, but to those of other cultures and other civilizations, too. Other men in other climes have asked themselves the same basic questions we have, and sometimes different ones, too, but in answer to them they have come up with sets of symbols and values which structure a life meaningful to them in utterly different ways than those to which we are

The University and the Inmost Life of Man

accustomed. Why? What are those symbolic forms, those configurations of values, so foreign to us, yet so meaningful and satisfying to them? Why do they provide answers? How do they differ from ours? How are they similar? What can we learn from them in order to penetrate man's inmost life from directions and in ways yet undreamed of by us? The university, if it wants to help man get at himself in depth, will have to do much more in the study of world religions. With some few honorable exceptions of long duration, we have barely begun to provide this help.

In summary so far: we are participants in a world wherein there has been a phenomenal growth in our knowledge of the physical universe, of man and his life world, a world wherein we have both exteriorized and interiorized knowledge, a world wherein we are increasingly involved in an organized thrust into the future and wherein we see the ever-increasing possibilities of creating and re-creating the internal and external conditions of our own human lives. With all this we are also increasingly aware of the responsibilities that such a future brings with it. We cannot be remiss then in trying to provide some of the help that man seeks not only for the ultimate meaning behind all this, but also, and more importantly to him, for the ultimate meaning of his own person. The systems of ultimate values that man has structured must be part of the university's concern for knowledge. Such systems most often take the form of religions and their intellectual elaboration which we know as theology. Therefore, the university must take into its ambit not only philosophy but also theology and all that it embraces in the form of systems of belief, systems of conduct, and systems of worship as a proper object of intellectual endeavors in study and research.

How this or any university should, in practice, go about such a concern in its concrete details it would, of course, be presumptuous of me to say. Nor could I tell a university how it was to structure or set up its investigation of the physical universe in a chemistry or physics department, nor how it should organize its psychology courses to deal with that aspect of man and his environment. But just as I am sure that the university *must* so investigate man and his world in physics or psychology, so am I sure that it must investigate man and his world in theology and religious studies of whatever type they might be.

Now we come to what seems to me to be the most difficult part of the role of the university in its relation to the inmost life of man. A university is research laboratories and library holdings and classrooms and curriculum plans and, God help us, administrative and educational budgets, and . . . you could carry on the list as long as I. It is also work on the highest level of intellectual competence. But it is people, persons, in all the uniqueness and interrelatedness of personality in its manifestations and in its roots, who use the laboratories, read the books, teach the classes. Everything said so far is meaningless unless kept in the living context of the persons who make up the university community.

As a person, I seek not only the abstract what or why of meaning or value, not only the universal literary types of love and sorrow and duty and worship, not only the history of philosophy, not only the psychology of religion. I seek the what and why of meaning and value for *myself*. I experience love and sorrow and the ambiguity of duty and the ecstasy and the dark night of worship. I so experience life and the questions it brings, and so do the other members of the university, each in his own way.

Complicated as this is, it is seen to be even more so when we remember that the members of the university are not simply isolated individuals in a haphazard or even in an extrinsically ordered conglomerate. They, we, constitute a community. No matter the different explanations of how the university constitutes this community; it is undeniably so conceived by its members. Indeed, today more than ever, it is praised when the perceived reality lives up to the conception, and it is often damned when protestations of community fail to square with the reality of fragmentation and isolation.

Without wishing to encroach on another of the subjects of this symposium, the needs of the students, still one cannot seriously consider the university's responsibility to the inmost life of man without seeing it in the context of university person in university community. It is a community of scholar and apprentice, teacher and student, older and younger person. Each is susceptible to the presence of the other. Each member of this community is engaged in the venture of education not only in the imparting of formal instruction in classroom and laboratory, but just as much in the confrontation of each by the other, in an almost numberless variety of images of man. It is the unique response of every learner (whether student or professor, younger or older) to such images of man which he encounters that draws out of him, educes from him, his own personal potentialities, and thus educates him insofar as he makes tradition his own and, in his person, carries it on in his own unique way into the future.

Here the student, the younger person in this community, seems to have a special advantage and a special problem. For as Ortega y Gasset once remarked: "Life consists in giving up the state of availability. Mere availability is the characteristic of growth faced with maturity. The youth, because he is not yet anything determinate and irrevocable, is everything potentially. Herein lies his charm and his insolence. Feeling that he is everything potentially, he supposes that he is everything actually."[1] It is the advantage of the younger person that his personal vocation is still before him, his self is still open to being fashioned. It is his problem that such an openness leaves him vulnerable. He is vulnerable to a

[1] José Ortega y Gasset, "In Search of Goethe from Within," *The New Partisan Reader,* 1945–1953, William Phillips and Philip Rahv, editors (New York, 1953), p. 289.

counterfeit structure or to the refusal to structure his life at all. He is most vulnerable to the dehumanizing and demoralizing effects of disillusionment with a community and its members who profess knowledge but ignore wisdom, who discourse learnedly but live meanly, who commune with the great minds of the past and expound the great discoveries of the present but who refuse to respond to the questing *persons* of the present and sneer at or, worse, ignore their hopes for the future.

If for the young this is how the university appears to them, is it any wonder that they react as they do? For so many there is nowhere else to look for ultimate personal answers; they come to the university in search of them and not finding even a personal concern for them or their quest they turn despairingly against a structure which to them seems a fraud.

On the other hand, the teacher in such a community has a special opportunity and responsibility. His it is in the first place to present in his teaching, but even more in his life, the concrete options, the real possibilities, the incarnated actualities which are among the varied images of man, and in encounter with which the student can structure his own self. The response to our potentialities lies only within, at the very deepest interior of ourselves. But the call comes from without. We truly know that we *can* be only in what we actually *are* in our response to each new situation.

If the old institutions, the old, inherited structures of family and church and nation and culture, often enough today seemingly cannot provide for society and especially for the young, the future of society, the situations and much less the answers wherein they find images of authentic man, perhaps the university can, as a shared community of learning and meaning. We all know that a university cannot tell its members *how* to think. We also know that it has a long history of *helping* them to think. I would suggest that the university should do more: it should *help* the student, it should help all its members, to *think and* to *feel* about matters of importance.

It can only do this in a shared contact with the lived concerns of those members. That is all very well in the abstract. In the concrete it means that the university should provide structures for such sharing, from more sympathetic faculty and administrators to less barracks passing for residence halls, from availability of counselling to specific involvement in our urban ghettoes, from a physical environment if not of beauty at least of harmony to defense of unpopular dissent. In the concrete it means the university taking seriously Plato's remark that the unexamined life is not worth living. It means the university living in its members a critical life, informed, regardful of facts, generous and intelligent, but also willing to analyze, examine, study, evaluate not only our society at large or even the university at large. That is too easily what Dickens calls "telescopic philanthropy." Such a shared contact in the living concern of the members means such generous and critical examination and evaluation of

The University and the Inmost Life of Man

ourselves too as university persons, as persons simply. How often does the university community help its members to think and to feel about matters of importance? How often does it help a man to grow in the capacity for a truly moral judgement, a response of the whole person to a particular situation? How often is the university even aware that for the young today the great need is for communities of vision and sustenance, and that today perhaps the university is the one community which might provide this?

No university of itself, or in its courses, or in its members can give a perfectly complete or adequate image of man, either in the conceptual and abstract description of the human condition such as in philosophy, or in ideal types such as in sociology, or even in the more concrete representations of a great work of literature. No one of these will ever represent of or by itself authentic human existence. But then, of course, there is no such thing as a generalized human existence. There is simply *man,* recognized in myself, in other men, and in and through the concrete, unique, single persons who realize their humanity by responding to the call of others in the one, unique, personal way that each of them can do so. Each of us structures his own image of man. Each does so in his moral life by the combination of the demand placed upon him by what is other than himself and by his unique response to that demand. Each does it in part alone and in part ineluctably bound up with his life communities. Each of us is in a search to understand himself in order that he might become himself. Each of us looks for an authentic and personal humanity which is true both to all that is common to man and unique to me.

All men do this. André Malraux once said that: "The greatest mystery is not that we have been flung at random among the profusion of the earth and the galaxy of the stars, but that in this prison we can fashion images sufficiently powerful to deny our nothingness."[2]

No man does this by himself, and the same reasons, mentioned earlier, which have today made of the university a unique help to man in his search for truth also obtain for man in his search for meaning. On the other hand, any university committed to man fully as he is will have to play its role in this part of man's task, too.

If this is applicable to any university, and I submit that it is, then it is even more applicable to a committed university. Of course, such a university can conceive of the carrying out of its commitment in a propagandistic way, in the arbitrary closing out of options, in the construction of a fully-answered universe, in the fashioning of a ready-to-wear image of man. But then it is not a university and need not at all concern us here. Even a University committed to the Christian faith can so act. But then it too,

---

[2] André Malraux, *"The Walnut Trees of Altenberg"* in Maurice Friedman, *To Deny Our Nothingness,* (New York, 1967), p. 17.

whatever else it might be, is not a university. So let us pass it by also.

On the other hand, a university committed to the Christian faith can, first, recognize openly and indeed joyfully that every man so fashions images and so fashions himself in the demands of the other and in his unique response to such demands. Secondly, it can with equal joy and openness present to him in its own contemporary witness to Christ one who is totally other, God Himself, and who thus makes total demands, and yet one who has in his unique response to those demands of the other fulfilled all of his own potentialities for truth, for meaning and for personhood. In turn, Christ and the Christian witness is not a fixed model or set pattern. Rather, we would say that Christ is our best encounter, the one in which we have the best possibility of fashioning our own unique response of truth, of meaning and of personhood.

In the inmost life of man, as Raymond Nogar has said, "it is not the events of time and space which make all the difference, as though the cosmos were providentially unfolding like a great machine, grinding out human destiny in accordance with unalterable laws. It is the value which you as a free and creative person assign to the things that happen."[3]

Today the university has an opportunity unlike that of any earlier time. As a company of scholars

[3] Raymond J. Nogar, O.P., *The Lord of the Absurd* (New York, 1966), p. 32.

over the past centuries it has shared in the remaking of man's vision of the world. As a *community* of scholars, mature and apprentice, it can share even more fully in the remaking of man's vision of his *interior* world. It can, if rightly structured, help man not only to think deeply but also to feel deeply about matters of importance. It can help provide the atmosphere in which values can be assigned freely and creatively to our circumstances. Insofar as it helps us to bear the twin and personal responsibilities of truth and meaning, the university will become fully *it*self as we become fully *our*selves in our inmost life.

THE UNIVERSITY—FOUNTAINHEAD OF KNOWLEDGE

Lee A. DuBridge

WHEN I VISIT ANY UNIVERSITY, I ALWAYS FEEL A pang of regret, a sense of longing, for I always wish that I were a student again.

I have lived in the world of higher education ever since I was a college freshman nearly fifty years ago. But how wonderful it would have been if I could have spent *all* of those years just as a student! I know that this is an impossible wish: in the modern world anyone who remained a student for fifty years, even if he could afford it, would be despised as a parasite on society. But suppose that, as a freshman, I could have looked forward to fifty years of learning instead of only four, or of eight if I took a Ph.D. What a course of study I could have laid out for myself!

I would have spent the first six or eight years studying mathematics and physics and chemistry. I would have learned all I possibly could about the nature of matter and of energy, about atoms and molecules and light and electricity and gravity. I would want to know how the nucleus is put together, and how it can be split apart, and how so much energy can be packed away in it.

After all this, I would move into astronomy and learn about the universe—the planets, the stars, the galaxies, the mysterious quasars. Why do the stars shine? How long have they been shining? How much longer will they last—and then what will happen? How did the universe begin? Will it ever end? How did our solar system originate? What is the earth itself really like and how did it get that way?

This would lead at once to the question of how life originated on earth. What is life? What is its chemical nature? How does evolution take place? How and why do various life forms originate, flourish for a time, and then possibly die out? What is the mysterious process we call heredity? This, of course, would lead to the question of man. How did he originate? How does he differ from other animals? How did he come to be able to ask questions about himself and about the universe? What is the nature of the thing he calls his brain? How does man think and feel, be sad or happy, imagine new things, create poetry and paintings, build great and beautiful structures?

Obviously, to find any answers I would be studying archeology, history, art, literature, music, philosophy, religion, sociology, economics, government— the whole spectrum of human ideas and institutions.

Would anybody doubt that I could easily spend

The University: Fountainhead of Knowledge

fifty years studying about the universe and about man and still not know all I would like to know?

The only trouble is that I would never make it. Why? For one simple reason: If I really were intent on learning all there was to know about physics, for example, or astronomy, or biology, or economics, or philosophy, I would soon come to some questions for which *nobody* had any answers. How many elementary particles are there? Nobody knows. How big is the universe? Nobody knows. How does the DNA molecule govern the development of a newborn creature? No one fully knows. Why do men and nations always fight each other? Why does our social and economic system not insure a good life for everyone?

We do not know! *We do not know!*

If I were really the inquisitive type of scholar I am now imagining myself to be, I would not be satisfied with all these expressions of ignorance. Sooner or later I would say: Well, if we don't know, *let us find out*. And so, inevitably, I would ditch my plans for future study and I would join forces with some scholar who was seeking the answers to some of these questions, and whom I would like to help. If there is ignorance here, I would like to push the barrier of ignorance back just a little. Instead of just absorbing knowledge for the rest of my life, I would like to help *advance* knowledge just a little bit.

No one could be a student forever. If he were so much interested in learning, he would soon become a professor. And, as a professor, he would have the pleasure of imparting some of what he knew to his students, *and,* at the same time he would be seeking to extend knowledge in his favorite field, seeking to find answers to questions to which no answers are known.

That is what a university is. It is a community of people, inquisitive people, seeking answers to important questions. Some seek answers just to satisfy their curiosity. Some are trying to learn things which will fit them for a business or profession. Others seek a deeper understanding of human problems so they can go out and help solve them by building better schools, better cities, a better government.

But a university is the gathering place for people interested in knowledge—knowledge that other people have, or knowledge that no one yet has.

Now many students seem to think that the acquisition of knowledge is just an unpleasant chore forced by the older generation on the younger generation, a chore to be put behind as quickly as possible.

Yet, there *are* deeper motivations. The desire for knowledge and understanding is, in fact, the overriding urge and the outstanding characteristic of that species of life we call *Homo sapiens.* Man is a man because he can learn, because he can understand, and he *wants* to learn and understand. Man is not a man just because he knows a lot; he is a man because he knows that he knows too little and he wants to learn more. Men are men because they know knowledge is useful, even necessary. They are

The University: Fountainhead of Knowledge

men even more when they know that learning is their birthright, that understanding is their greatest destiny.

All of this, of course, is just a roundabout way of saying that the university, as a center of teaching and learning, as a center of scholarship and research, a center of knowledge and understanding, is one of the great social institutions of civilized man. Society as we know it exists because of the knowledge and understanding which men have attained. Society the world over will improve only as our understanding and our wisdom increase.

Do we really know and appreciate this in America? Or do we think of the university more as a production line to turn out skilled manpower, or a necessary step to business success and social acceptance? Or do we think of the university as a mechanism for social stability or even of social change, a service station or a department store to provide practical services to the community or the nation and to give students a chance to taste a little of this and a little of that? Or do we join those who believe it to be a refuge for rebellious students and crazy professors or just a mechanism for keeping nearly half our young people off the labor market for four years without having to list them as unemployed?

Or does the word "university" create an image of a place where the government spends millions of dollars a year on useless research, coddling a bunch of professors who have nothing better to do than to play with cyclotrons and electron microscopes, study sea urchins or fruit flies or bread mold, make smelly chemicals, or hike in the mountains to find pretty rocks, or propose radical new ideas about economics or government?

The university is many things to many people. It is or does some of the things I have mentioned. But if the American people think of the university *only* in these terms, they have missed the point.

Unfortunately I think that we as a people have missed the point. We do not understand the purpose of the university as a fountainhead of knowledge. We do not understand the university as striving to fulfill the highest aspirations of man as a thinking animal, the aspiration to know and to understand. We forget even the age-old truths that knowledge is power, that the truth shall make you free, that ignorance is the enemy of all that men hold dear, that the troubles of the world stem not from knowledge, but from ignorance.

True, no university is perfect, nor is any human institution. There are idle, thoughtless and rebellious students to be found, as well as careless and superficial teachers or incompetent administrators. But, over all, the history of the achievements of higher education in Europe and in America is a glorious one. It can be more glorious in the future than in the past, but not if the university forgets its primary purpose; and not if the society which benefits from the university's work does not understand its purpose and match its understanding with adequate support.

There are many aspects of the university which

The University: Fountainhead of Knowledge

people fail to understand, such as some of the misconceptions already mentioned. But one area of misunderstanding gives me great concern—the relation between teaching and research. I hope that I have clearly stated the basic truth: teaching (or learning) and research are two aspects of the same thing: the search for knowledge and of understanding, the search for truth.

A student comes to a university presumably to learn the things that other great men have learned and taught over the centuries. A professor, when he enters his research laboratory or study, is seeking truths that no one has yet uncovered. They have a common objective, a common yearning. The university is their meeting ground, always has been and always will be. Research laboratories without students tend to grow sterile; teachers who are not scholars become sterile, too. The young student and the mature scholar profit from each other immensely. It is a sad thing when this mutual dependence is not appreciated on both sides, as I know it sometimes is not. I often wonder why professors who do not like students ever remain in a university and why students who do not want to be taught by scholars ever go there in the first place. But the very fact that universities persist in our society proves that this basic community of interest is a very powerful force. The great university is the home of the great scholar and the perceptive student is attracted to it as to a magnet. We in the university world must understand this powerful magnetism; we must also explain it to others.

The great shortcoming of universities today is not that they have too many active research scholars, but too few. There are not enough to go around, and we could not afford to hire them if there were. If we could afford to have one professor for every five students instead of one for every ten or twenty, our universities would be greater places for both faculty and students. And they would become greater fountainheads for knowledge, thus benefiting our whole society. But until more scholars are trained, or more money is found, or fewer students want to go to college, we shall have to do the best we can, although we all wish it could be better.

It will be better when our whole university world —students, faculty, alumni, and administrators— and our whole society—from workers to Congressmen—fully appreciate that the university is the fountainhead of knowledge, and for this reason also the fountainhead of civilized living for all people.

This year of our Lord, 1967, is an unhappy time here in America and in many other places in the world. Why? Is the world a much worse place now than it was in 1842, when the University of Notre Dame was founded? Or three hundred years ago when modern science had scarcely been born? Or five hundred years ago when poverty, disease, suffering, slavery or serfdom, despotism and cruel wars were the rule and not the exception?

The world is *better* than it ever was. But human

The University: Fountainhead of Knowledge

beings have learned more and understand more about the universe and about themselves. They know, therefore, that the world *can* be a better place in which to live, and that our unhappiness results from our own failure to *realize* our rising expectations. Such unhappiness is healthy if it enhances our determination to make things better, if it increases our efforts to learn more and to use our knowledge more effectively. The university in America can be a prime mover in advancing our understanding of, and seeking solutions to, the urgent problems that lie before us.

So much, then, for setting forth the ideals which any university must seek. We all know, however, that setting forth ideals is one thing and formulating practical programs to achieve these ideals is another. Every university worthy of the name has ideals which are, I am sure, consistent with those which I have been setting forth. Each university, however, must find its own mechanism and establish its own policies for striving to become, in its own way, a real fountainhead of knowledge.

It would be presumptuous of anyone to try to indicate to any particular university just what policies and practices it should adopt in its own program of combining its teaching and research functions to the best advantage. The impressive thing about the university system in America is its diversity. Many universities employ many practices, seeking essentially the same ends. To suggest that all universities adopt the same policies and practices would be to suggest a regimentation which would destroy the valuable independence of each and every institution.

It is true, of course, that government agencies require certain uniform practices on the part of the universities pertaining to their fiscal, accounting, contractual and reporting procedures. It is understandable that the government should seek certain uniformity in these respects, though it is also understandable that many universities find it difficult to adapt their procedures to these government rules. We can tolerate government regulations on fiscal procedures, though we must resist those which impinge in a vital way on the institution's freedom to pursue its own academic policies and goals.

However, I am not concerned with fiscal and accounting procedures. I am concerned about the way a university seeks to retain or enhance its position as a vigorous, progressive fountainhead of knowledge. I believe there are certain broad policies on which most universities agree. By agreeing on certain basic principles, the universities as a group can present a more united front to the American public and can thereby collectively assist each other in maintaining the essential ingredients of our academic integrity. Let me list a few of these areas of broad policy agreement.

1. *Scholarly research is an essential element of the educational enterprise.*

I have emphasized my strong belief that the concept of the university as a fountainhead of knowl-

The University: Fountainhead of Knowledge

edge implies that the university has responsibility for both the dissemination and the advancement of knowledge. I have indicated my belief that these two activities are mutually related and mutually dependent. This mutual dependence becomes especially clear when we consider graduate study, and graduate study is, after all, the activity which makes a university a *university* rather than a college. Graduate study *is* training in scholarly research, and graduate education is impossible without scholarly activity by both graduate students and faculty. It seems to follow that when a university chooses the research enterprises in which it wishes to engage, its first criterion for their desirability will be the contribution made to the total educational program. The purpose of a university research program is not to satisfy the whims of its professors, not to attract more dollars into the treasury—which will immediately flow out again—not even, particularly for a private institution, to render a service to the community. University research is an educational activity, and research activities which have no educational value could usually be done better in a nonuniversity agency.

It is true that in these times universities, or associations of universities, are often involved in special services to the state or federal government in managing off-campus research and development enterprises which are somewhat disconnected from the educational process. Special requirements and historical situations may make this type of management activity a desirable or necessary function for certain institutions. My own institution happens to be one, since we manage for the National Aeronautics and Space Administration the large Jet Propulsion Laboratory, several miles from the campus, conducting unclassified research and development relating to the exploration of the planetary system. These so-called "research centers" are in a special category and I shall disregard them in my discussion of university research as such.

2. The government support of research.

Since World War II various government agencies have engaged to a very substantial extent in the support of university campus-type research in basic sciences and in applied science. This support is gradually being extended into the social sciences, the arts and the humanities.

I think it is right, proper and necessary that both state and federal government agencies should support scholarly research in universities, both because the advance of knowledge contributes to the national welfare and because the education of graduate students is an important enterprise for the entire nation.

There are many people who misunderstand the attitudes and policies which government agencies have adopted in the support of university research. It is widely believed that such research projects are pressed upon universities as a special service to the government agency involved. In some cases, particularly with the off-campus research centers, this has indeed been the case. By and large, however, the

The University: Fountainhead of Knowledge

bulk of research supported by the federal government is research initiated within the university itself —research chosen to fit the educational policies of the institution and research carried out with the collaboration of graduate students and with an important educational objective in view. As long as each university restricts itself to proposals which embody these objectives, the federal support of such research, like the support by any other agency, public or private, is wholly proper, desirable and necessary. The advance of knowledge can well be taken as a necessary and proper *major* national goal.

There has been much misunderstanding about the fact that government agencies within the Department of Defense also support university research. In the years following World War II the Office of Naval Research was in fact the pioneer in initiating the support of the kinds of basic research which universities themselves wished to undertake and carry on. The policies of ONR have been widely adopted by other government agencies and have, on the whole, been a fine model for proper relations between a government agency and a university. Research supported by ONR and by other similar defense department agencies has generally not been secret or classified, and has generally not been related to the development of weapons of war. These agencies respond to the requests from the universities themselves and it is up to the universities to determine their policies regarding the areas and the kinds of research they desire to do. I do not myself favor conducting weapons research or any kind of secret or proprietary research on a university campus since this is inimical to the essential educational objective of a university. Most universities follow this principle, but there are special occasions where universities have thought it desirable and proper to carry on classified research. Now when a university does this in clear recognition of the policy elements involved, I think it is not up to those of us outside of that particular university to level criticism.

3. Private support of university research.

No university, however, could depend upon federal sources to support all of its scholarly activities. There is not enough government money to go around to do this (government policies in any case do not pay the full costs of such research) and there are many areas of scholarly endeavor appropriate to a university for which no government support has been established.

I personally favor the extension of government support of valid university scholarly research into fields not now encompassed in existing government programs. I refer particularly to areas in the social sciences, the arts and the humanities, and to certain areas of pure and applied science not now adequately covered.

At the same time I am a firm believer in the desirability of spreading widely the support of research by private sources or, in the case of public institutions, through state appropriations. Generous as many private foundations, individuals and corporations have been, I still believe that the promotion of high-quality university research aimed at the advancement of knowledge and the education of students is so important that it deserves far greater support from the private sector. Business and industrial corporations do make contributions to universities and in many cases these are most generous, and in all cases are most welcome. But American industry would be making an excellent investment if it could multiply several times over its support of scholarly investigations which are pertinent to its own fields of interest and which are valuable to the enhancement of the welfare of the community and the nation.

There are many areas of scholarly activity which it is unlikely that the federal government will, or possibly ever should, support. Private funds are essential for these areas, indeed are essential in all areas, to supplement government funds and to fill in the gaps which government funding involves, and especially to initiate those scholarly activities involving young scholars, brand-new ideas and possibly high-risk ventures.

4. Areas of danger.

Those of my generation can easily remember the days before World War II when scholarly research was a scandalously neglected activity in American universities. Few funds were available for it, university policies did not provide professors with adequate time for scholarly activities, and graduate instruction in any case was at a low level. It would be inevitable that the vast changes in this picture which have come about in the last twenty years would give rise to abuses and excesses. Some universities have regarded research activities as a prestige enterprise to be engaged in at all costs, even at the cost of a high-quality educational program for either graduates or undergraduates. To attract a professor into a university position with the incentive that he can spend all of his time in research and have no teaching is, I believe, a wholly improper perversion of the goals of university research, unless, of course, the individual is such a terrible teacher that he should not be allowed to come near the students. In this case he probably should not be in the university at all. Research has its place in the university, but it has such a place only if it is high-quality scholarly inquiry addressed to important and basic problems having to do with the nature of the universe, of man and of the society in which he lives; and if it is undertaken as a part of the educational program of the university and treated as a stimulus and support to that program. Undergraduates as well as graduates, should appreciate the opportunity of sitting at the feet of scholars who are working at the frontiers of the unknown, and should profit by it. Conversely, those working at the frontiers of the unknown should regard it as one of their great privileges to bring their students face to face with the problems that puzzle men and to encourage them to develop inquiring minds and to foster in them an unquenchable thirst for knowledge. Not all students

The University: Fountainhead of Knowledge

are interested or capable of acquiring this thirst; not all professors are capable of stimulating it. But so many do that it is clearly a realizable as well as an essential goal that this be the spirit which permeates the fountainheads of knowledge which we call our great universities.

These, then, are my feelings about the university as a center of knowledge. These are, I am sure, the policies followed at Notre Dame. But these do *not* represent the average citizen's view of a university, nor the average Congressman's view. We all have a job to do in understanding ourselves and then in conveying this understanding to others.

A great university system is one of the most precious assets which any nation can possess. The knowledge and the ideas that will create a better world tomorrow are being generated in our universities today.

THE UNIVERSITY AND THE LIFE OF THE STUDENT: THE NEXT ONE HUNDRED YEARS

Nevitt Sanford

IN FORECASTING THE FUTURE IT IS EASIER TO SPEAK in terms of what is possible and preferable rather than in terms of what is probable. It is hard to guess what will happen next year, or next century, but it is possible that by being clear about our preferences, and by working in their interests, we may help make them probable.

What started me thinking about the future was a television program director's proposal that I help prepare a half-hour show on "drugs in the year 2000." Was it not likely that by that time we would have drugs not only to create whatever mood we desired but to produce whatever personality traits we desired—to make people aggressive, submissive, creative or ambitious? I found myself replying, in a somewhat ill-humored way, that by the year 2000 it would be considered absurd to try to crowd a discussion of a complex or controversial subject into a half-hour television program; as for drugs, they would become generally boring long before that time. Then I had a fantasy, which I offered as the basis for a little television play. About 1994 a scientist produced what he believed was a true wonder drug, one that would neutralize the effects of all other drugs. But he could find no one willing to try it. People were afraid of what might happen if they lost the benefits of all the antibiotic, antihistamine, antidepression, antisuperego, and antinomian substances that had become parts of their daily intake. Finally, through the collaboration of several government agencies, a young man was persuaded to take the risk in exchange for release from his national service in Bechuanaland, where a rebellion had broken out. The results were, as the scientist expected, truly marvelous. The young man reported after the first day that he felt just great. The world was beautiful, his food delicious, his wife glamorous, the sound of children's voices delightful. His spirits soared. It happened that his football team lost that day, but he said, "It's not whether you won or lost, but how you played the game." But, alas, he survived for only three days. Without protection from microorganisms in the environment, he was doomed. Although air pollution had been more or less taken care of by the advent of the electric car, it had not become possible to enforce the meat inspection laws in his state.

This is my general view of the future: We will go pretty far in our fascination with chemistry and with

The University and the Life of the Student

machines and in the direction of identifying ourselves with them, but in time we will realize that we are nothing but men; and will, indeed, learn to take satisfaction in this fact, valuing what is distinctively human and seeing that our own humanity and that of other people must be realized together. The great excitement, in other words, will come from psychological progress.

When we have rediscovered our humanity we will have a basis for rebuilding our educational system. It is possible even now to envision a truly humanistic education that is devoted to the fullest possible development of the individual, that is available to everybody, and that will continue throughout each person's life.

But to see this vision realized we must first survive the present crisis of confidence. We must regain confidence in our ability as individuals and as a nation, to affect, in the interest of human values, the course of events on the world scene and to control our technology. We are at present on a course of empire building and of uncontrolled technology. Essentially, our empire building is borne on an indescribably powerful technology that is still guided by nineteenth-century economic theory and a tribal conception of relations among people. The problem is to learn how to distribute the fruits of our technology and how to avoid ascribing to other nations faults that lie within ourselves.

I say it is *possible* that this crisis will be resolved. But I admit that this will be a bootstrap operation.

A resolution depends on the very education that I see flowering in the future, education that will enable man to become, increasingly, master of himself.

Gaining control of our technology is essentially a psychological matter. Machines and their works, and machinelike ways of organizing human activity, will always be with us. It will be our task to relate to them in ways that do not diminish our humanity; hopefully, in ways that will serve our distinctively human needs.

The important thing here is to be clear about where *we* leave off and the technological aids begin. No one can deny the advantages of our using machines to increase the power and accuracy of our muscular operations, of using media to improve our senses and computers to assist our mental activities, certainly not as long as we ourselves are the major determiners of what happens. The trouble comes when we begin to identify ourselves with our technology. A man may act toward his sports car or motor bike as if it were in fact a part of himself; or he may lose the distinction between himself and his role in a work organization.

There is irony in the fact that the hippie culture seems to have invented the expression "turned on," which suggests that its user might think of himself as an electrical appliance. There was in fact a little boy, an autistic child, who believed that he was run by electricity and lived in terror that someone would unplug him.

There is also danger in the tendency to endow

technological phenomena such as the Bomb with human qualities or identities, as when such a phenomenon comes to symbolize a parent of one's childhood and is loved or hated as was that parent.

This kind of relations with technology is dehumanizing. And there is reason to believe that those who take part in them become inclined to see other people as less than human, that is, as machines or objects. Probably this is most likely to happen when the machine or technological phenomenon is understood little or not at all. But since there is little likelihood that very many people can fully understand our increasingly complex technological achievements, the best safeguard against dehumanization is an education for self-awareness, self-determination, and mature self-esteem.

Such an education, with the accent on self-awareness, is also our best hope of achieving a more equitable distribution of the products of technology, thus reducing conflicts among nations and among groups within the nation. Feeding the peoples of the world does not seem to be beyond the powers of technology, but finding the will to do it is another matter. In a time of plenty or superabundance, we cling to the idea that people must work for what they get (that is, poor people should, not necessarily stockholders), because we have not completely mastered our own greed and laziness. We need to control other peoples because we are not sure we can control ourselves. We need to believe there are people fundamentally different from ourselves; we need them to represent what we are not supposed to do and to stand as embodiments of reprehensible tendencies we cannot recognize in ourselves.

These basic psychological problems will yield only to a humanizing education.

Once again, then, we are involved in a race between education and catastrophe. The outcome seems in doubt, but it is possible that education will win. Otherwise, there might be little future to talk about and my presentation would end at this point.

The above is an argument for the proposition that individual development is the most fundamental educational goal. If we resolve the present crises this goal will be generally accepted. We will then find in the past much that is usable. We will then recognize that Socrates, who urged us to know ourselves, and Jesus, who said "love thy neighbor as thyself," set us on the right path.

Other aims of education, which are chiefly that of inducting the individual into the life and spirit of his culture and thus preserving it, and that of preparing him to contribute to the productive work of his society, will be seen as interrelated with, but largely dependent upon, the primary aim. Although the formation of personality owes much to culture which each individual assimilates in his own way, and to vocational training which may expand the individual's abilities and help him to define himself, the preservation and further enrichment of our culture will depend most heavily upon highly developed individuals. And it is only the developed individual who can adapt himself creatively and productively to the rapidly changing requirements of the world of work. In sum, it is only through becoming psychologically developed that a person may maintain his humanity, participate fully in the benefits of a complex culture, and be truly useful to society.

A major function of personality theory, which will become highly developed and well-understood by educators in the years ahead, is to help clarify the developmental aims of education, and to state them in terms that will permit us to see their interrelations and the ways in which they depend upon educational policies and procedures.

Our love of our neighbor, to take an example, increases with our knowledge of him, but it also depends on our knowledge of ourselves, for if we are blind to our own weaknesses and aggressive impulses we may easily attribute them to our neighbor and make them grounds for hating him. Our love of our neighbor also depends on our love of ourselves —love in the sense of respect and acceptance—for self-contempt and self-doubt make us selfish and egotistical, and unable to give anything to a neighbor. But to know ourselves we must be loved by others; otherwise we would lack the confidence that self-examination requires; and in order to love ourselves with full knowledge of ourselves, we need to be regarded with understanding and compassion. It follows from this that when we love our neighbor we help him to achieve self-knowledge.

In all this it seems that modern personality theory and the wisdom of the ancients can easily be brought into harmony. The question is how, precisely, may we plan an educational environment that will encourage development toward the high goals that have been envisioned? In the future, this planning will be done in accord with knowledge of how young people actually develop. It will be understood that the personality is a whole whose interacting features—abilities, feelings, traits of character—develop through graded challenges and through experiences that give self-insight. In this perspective it will become clear that the learning of set bodies of content is far from being the heart of the educational process and may be a barrier to genuine education. While it will be assumed that everybody should have some familiarity with his culture, and that communication in a social group is favored by shared knowledge, it will be recognized that where individual development is concerned the same end may be reached through the use of quite different materials.

Thus, in undergraduate education, subject matter will be chosen, not with a view to keeping up with the so-called explosion in knowledge, but on the basis of its usefulness in the hands of the particular teacher as a means for developing intellectual powers, or acquainting the student with his feelings, or offering him the symbols that will permit him to find satisfaction of his inner emotional needs in the realm of the imagination.

Freed from the grim compulsion to cover content,

The University and the Life of the Student

teachers will be able to teach well, to get on with the really important business of helping students to make sense of their own experiences and observations. Teachers will also be free to get to know their students and will find them interesting; they will see that a little encouragement or a little firmness at the right time can be crucial to the student's progress toward maturity. And students will have a chance to know their teachers as persons and to find in some of them, we may hope, models of committed intelligence and humane feeling. With the teaching of facts seen in its proper perspective, some of the technological aids to education, such as programmed instruction and talking typewriters, will recede very much into the background. Others, such as instructional television, films, and tapes to be inserted into television sets, which can present the person *and* his ideas and facts in a context of feeling and value, will continue to be of considerable importance. However, these will not replace the book or the printed word, which will remain the greatest technological aid to education, the greatest stimulus to the use of one's own imagination.

Far more than at present, education will take place in various settings other than institutional classrooms—at home, in the streets, at museums, fairs, public events, at places of work, during forty-five-minute coffee breaks, at pubs, resort hotels—wherever people gather and life is lived. Churches will be particularly important as educational centers. They will, in fact, long before the year 2000 have staged something of a comeback. Guided by new prophetic leadership and the ecumenical spirit they will become major centers for the development of the whole man. They will deliberately bring together what schools and colleges have been at pains to separate—knowledge of one area and knowledge of another, art and science, thought and feeling, inquiry and action—and people of different ages.

At the same time, however, there will still be institutions not unlike the colleges and universities of today. Giant universities will persist for the foreseeable future, for they will be needed as centers for research and training. Some educational activities will still go on there, but we will not have vast numbers of undergraduates being processed in systems of departments, courses, and grades. With set arrangements of content de-emphasized, undergraduate education will be freed from domination by departments, and undergraduate populations will be divided into subgroups small enough to permit the formation of close communities.

Indeed, all educational institutions will have become genuine communities, for it will be well understood that individual development depends upon the total environment of the school, college, or university.

It will generally be understood that in order to be good communities these institutions must base themselves upon certain values that are basic to democratic society. Chief among these, I think, are trust, love, justice, freedom, and truth. We take these val-

The University and the Life of the Student

ues for granted and they are rarely mentioned in discussions of educational environments; yet it must be said that they are often ignored or neglected or even directly countered today by institutions bent on survival, or power, or success, or reputation. There are colleges that will turn most of their students into slaves and most of their faculty members into bureaucrats in order to do something called "raising standards."

Without trust there can be no community, for each man in an aggregation of people would regard every other as his enemy; unless he can trust someone the infant cannot grow beyond psychological infancy, and unless he is trusted the adolescent cannot become adult. Yet there are colleges in which the students do not trust the faculty, the faculty do not trust the students, and nobody trusts the president.

No one can become fully human unless he is loved and loves someone else; no one will have any impulse to help others or to contribute to his community unless he is allowed to feel he is worth something, unless he knows he will be the object of concern and care when he is in trouble; yet there are institutions of higher learning in which students feel they are valued only for their academic achievements and faculty feel they are valued only for their publications.

Without justice men become aggressive and cynical, and in time they take up positions outside the system that has denied them; yet there are colleges and universities in which students are required to abide by rules they had no part in making and have not accepted, and in which the system for promoting faculty members is grossly unfair.

We need freedom in order to develop ourselves and to be ourselves. The highly developed person is a freely choosing person; his ability to choose depends on his having had opportunities to make choices, and his actual choosing requires an environment that offers genuine alternatives; yet there are colleges in which the freedom of students is much too restricted by internal pressures of tradition, authority, or educational fashion, perhaps of student peer groups that educators do nothing to counter, or by external pressures from alumni, parents, religious groups, state legislators, or the man in the street whose simplistic or moralistic ideas about education are not challenged by the college administration.

Truth, of course, is the overriding value, particularly in institutions of higher learning. It is the basis for our control of ourselves and of our environment. I have no doubt that universities are making great progress toward the discovery and dissemination of the truth about the physical and organic worlds; indeed it often seems that other high values are sacrificed to this end; but to know ourselves and the social world—this is something else. Self-knowledge may be opposed by our wishes, and knowledge of society may threaten the interests of powerful groups. Not surprisingly, there are colleges in which virtually nothing is done to give students insight into themselves, and where major social hypotheses cannot be entertained.

The point here is that the successful pursuit of truth about self and society depends upon all the other values just considered. Indeed it seems that these values, though they interact in various ways, fall into a hierarchy. Truth depends on freedom (if we are not permitted to think about any one thing all our thinking is impaired), but men will not care about freedom unless they have justice, and in order to develop sufficiently to be sensitive on this point they need love and trust. There is a suggestion here as to how the college president might sort out his priorities.

But my concern is with the future, not with the somewhat grim present. In the future, long before 2042, we will have clarified our values and their interrelations and will have learned to put first things first, perhaps along the lines just suggested. This will be due not only to a change of heart among educators but also to important changes in their circumstances. Universities will have become fully aware of the power they already have: they provide the knowledge base for our technology and can as well become cornerstones for social reconstruction; and with each student subsidized by the government—as they will be—private colleges will not have to sell their souls in order to survive.

Although most undergraduate institutions will, before 2042, exhibit the basic features of a good community, they will nevertheless differ among themselves in some important ways. For one thing, there will be different conceptions of the highly developed individual and of how he is formed, even though the general goal of individual development will be universally shared. More than this, colleges will differ in size and in their relationships to their surrounding communities, in their curricula, and in the composition of their student and faculty bodies.

With respect to size and location, there will be colleges of 300 to 600 students located within universities—the "cluster college" idea having become fully accepted—and there will be large community colleges; there will be small colleges located in metropolitan areas maintaining their own identity through being residential, and deliberately developing a culture of their own, while their students take most of their course work at nearby universities; there will be colleges of a new kind located in large cities, colleges where students make their own arrangements for living but study an integrated curriculum organized around the problems of the metropolis. Colleges in relatively isolated areas will still exist but according to a new arrangement that has already made its appearance: a majority of the students and many of the faculty will spend more than half of their time away from the campus, studying abroad, taking part in organized work-study programs in the cities, in national service, and similar organizations, the campus itself being primarily a place for retreat and contemplation.

As for curricula, probably most of those known

The University and the Life of the Student

and used at present will still be in existence. It will be understood that each is best suited to some kinds of students, or to students in a certain stage of their development. It must be admitted, though, that some particular curricula will persist because some colleges will not have changed—colleges that have not changed during the *last* one hundred years. In general, however, all curricula will have changed in the direction of greater relevance to the life of the times.

Although ability tests of the sort now in common use will have been abandoned, there will still be a tendency for the brightest and most advantaged students to select, and be selected by, particular institutions. But most institutions will be relatively nonselective, having found ways to serve students of quite different ability levels and to reap the benefits of diversity. There will be special institutions designed for young people whose rate of development is relatively slow.

We will, long before 2042, not only be educating the whole person, but we will be educating all the people, both those in the 17 to 21 age range and those who have already had the benefits we now expect from four years of college. Education for the less able young people and for those who have been deprived will be continued through their teens; because of their relatively slow rates of development it may take so much time to bring them to a stage at which they can participate in the benefits of our society. We will offer this kind of education not because these young people must contribute to production—though it may be hoped that they will—but because they are our own.

This means that we will have given up the idea that education is a scarce commodity; we will be acting according to a belief in abundance. It will no longer be assumed that less able and less privileged people must work for what they get and be given vocational training from an early age, while the more privileged are encouraged to take a leisurely course through college and graduate school while making up their minds about their aims in life. All will be given a chance to develop their personalities, all will be taught to play as well as to work, and in time the distinction between these two types of activity will be far less clear than it is today.

This view of less privileged people will hold for the less developed and more populous countries of the world as well as for our own country; and the education of people in these other countries will become a major and a most rewarding activity of the best educated of our own young people.

The education of the less able, the emotionally and culturally handicapped, will require new programs and new institutions, planned according to knowledge of personality development. It will be understood, for example, that there are young people who cannot be taught basic skills until their self-conceptions have been changed to those of someone who *can* learn and until they have been induced to orient themselves toward the future. We will also understand from our knowledge of the order of

The University and the Life of the Student

events in human development how to put first things first; accordingly, we will teach children how to enjoy reading before we move on to social studies.

If you ask where we will get the people to man those new programs and institutions, the answer is that the bulk of them will be students in institutions much like our present colleges and universities, for it will be understood that helping with the education of others is among the best ways to educate ourselves.

As for adults, both those who have had college experience and those who have not, by the end of this century almost all will be spending an important part of their time in educational activity. This will be not only because people will need continuing education in order to keep pace with the changing requirements of their jobs, but because it will be understood that people may further develop themselves and enrich their lives at any age, and that this is to be done through activities that are educational in the larger meaning of the word.

While these activities will take place in various settings, many of them will be carried out in institutions much like our present schools, colleges, and universities. Present new construction looks as if it will last for more than a hundred years, and these structures will have to be put to use. With at least half of the college-age students away at any given time doing field work or occupying educational beachheads, spaces will be filled with adults of various ages. All school buildings will be at the same time community centers, with people of different ages doing the same things at the same time. This will reduce the "generation gap" and solve the problems created by "student power." And since all—adults or students or youth—will, whether in or out of institutions, be helping with the education of the less able of the world, we will have a truly human community, an educated and educating society.

Institutions will also differ because their faculties will have different needs and interests. Much as at present, there will be some institutions in which faculty members engage in research, public service, and teaching, with varying amounts of time being devoted to each of these kinds of activity; while in other institutions virtually all of the faculty will concentrate on teaching. In all institutions it will be seen that the development of the faculty is as important as that of the students, and that faculty and students alike benefit from membership in a truly human community.

The research that academic men do, particularly in the social sciences, will be related more closely than at present to the problems of the community. Action on these problems will be planned, and even carried out, by the men who study them; in other words, the roles of scientist and citizen will not be so sharply separated as they are at the present time.

Most college teachers will publish little or not at all; teaching itself will have become a well-rewarded, as it is a rewarding, profession. In addition, non-publication will be aided by a form of "knowledge

The University and the Life of the Student

control" or "birth-of-the-book control." Before the turn of the century it will be recognized that radical action is necessary to limit the outpouring of specialized and often trivial publications that even now all but inundate the offices of every academic man. The most prestigious colleges will begin by making rules forbidding their professors to publish until they have been on the faculty five or even ten years, and they will thus create a campus culture in which publishing is considered not good form. An exception, however, will be made in the case of "TV publication," an arrangement whereby a scientist or scholar who believes he has something important to say goes before the cameras to say it, in plain language, to the general public. These "TV publications" will, of course, be taken into consideration in the matter of promotion.

As the life of the faculty improves so will that of the student. With the faculty member's own needs being fulfilled and his morale on a high level, he will have the time and the inclination to give the student the care he needs.

In these circumstances both students and faculty will see that their needs for each other are only moderate. The main thing, from the point of view of the student, is assurance that the faculty is accessible. But the two groups will know each other well enough so that there will be no tendency for each to regard the other as alien, un-understandable, and probably hostile.

I am saying here that students need privacy as

well as sociability. With their privacy respected, and with relative freedom from the judgments and evaluations of an unknown faculty, students will be less competitive with each other and in a better position to develop meaningful and satisfying group relations.

Group solidarity will be based largely upon common purposes; the benefits now enjoyed by members of orchestras, choirs, and athletic teams will be enjoyed by students who join together in all kinds of artistic functions, social action, social service, and even scholarly activities. The student's knowledge that he can be of service to others will raise his self-esteem and put it on a sound basis, thus enabling him to reveal himself to others and thus to form deep and genuine relationships with others.

Since students of both sexes will join in these group activities young men and women will be able to know each other as people, to correct the stereotypes brought over from childhood, and thus to put an end to the dehumanized and dehumanizing patterns of dating and rating so common at the present time.

In the true community of the college or university and in the peer groups just described, the student will feel fully respected as a person; he will thus be able to accept himself as a developing person, able to enjoy the satisfactions and to assume the responsibilities appropriate to his age.

It all sounds very attractive. Must we wait for fifty or seventy-five years? Perhaps some fortunate institutions, with knowledge of what is required, can take giant steps toward the ideal right now.

THE VISION OF A GREAT CATHOLIC UNIVERSITY IN THE WORLD OF TODAY

Theodore M. Hesburgh, C. S. C.

ONE HUNDRED AND TWENTY-FIVE YEARS ARE NOT considered a very long time as the lives of great world universities are reckoned. I remember participating some years ago in the six hundredth anniversary of the University of Vienna. However, on the American scene, one hundred and twenty-five years are considered to be a respectable age. Relatively few American universities are older than we at Notre Dame today.

One should not make too much, however, of this matter of age. Age alone is no real guarantee of quality unless one is considering wine or cheese. Our present anniversary should be considered, I believe, rather as a grateful memorial to things past, an opportunity to assess things present, and, hopefully, as a look to the future. The proud and cherished traditions of the past, in a fast-moving and ever-changing world, should always be a prelude to what this University might yet become.

Theodore M. Hesburgh, C.S.C.

A look at today and tomorrow for this University must take into full account the specific challenges and opportunities that we particularly face as we ever try to create here at Notre Dame a great Catholic university. Also, we cannot avoid facing frankly the dangers and difficulties that confront us along this road of present and future development. But neither should we be timid, unimaginative, or defensive. In fact, what we need most at this juncture of our history are all the qualities of the pioneer: vision, courage, confidence, a great hope inspired by faith and ever revivified by love and dedication.

I hope that you are not shocked when I say that there has not been in recent centuries a truly great Catholic university, recognized universally as such. There are some universities that come very close to the reality, but not the full reality, at least as I see it in today's world. One might have hoped that history would have been different when one considers the Church's early role in the founding of the first great universities in the Middle Ages: Paris, Oxford, Cambridge, Bologna and others. They turned to the Church for the charters that would guarantee them a freedom and autonomy they could not then have had from the State. Knowledge grew quickly within them because there was that new atmosphere of the free and often turbulent clashing of conflicting ideas, where a man with a new idea, theological, philosophical, legal or scientific, had to defend it in the company of his peers, without interference from pressures and powers that neither create nor validate

The Vision of a Great Catholic University

intellectual activity, one of God's greatest gifts to man.

This medieval conjunction of the Church and the universities was to undergo a violent rupture in the years following the Reformation and, especially, the French Revolution. Philip Hughes, writing of this period, said: "Another grave loss was the disappearance of all the universities. They had been Catholic, and often Papal, foundations. In all of them there had been a faculty of theology, and round this mistress science their whole intellectual life had turned. Now they were gone, and when restored as State universities, (they became) academies for the exploration and exposition of natural truths alone. Education, the formation of the Catholic mind in the new Catholic Europe, would suffer immeasurably, and religious formation (would) be to its intellectual development an extra, something added on. There would be the further mischievous effect that henceforth not universities but seminaries would set the tone of theological life. The leaders of Catholic thought would not be the professional thinkers whom a university produces, but technicians, those to whom the important work of training the future clergy is committed and who, among other things, teach them theology. The effect of this destruction of the faculties of theology in the universities of Catholic Europe, the disappearance of the old Salamanca, Alcala, Coimbra, Bologna, Donai, Louvain and Paris, is a theme that still awaits its historian. Louvain was indeed restored in 1834, but the healthy interplay of the theological intellects of half a score of Catholic universities, the nineteenth century, was never, alas, to know."[1]

What we are trying to do today in creating great Catholic universities is, in a sense, a re-creation, so that the last third of the twentieth century will not suffer the loss which Philip Hughes bemoans for the nineteenth century and most of the twentieth. The comeback has begun in many places, Notre Dame being one of them. But this is happening in a much different world and in a much different climate of opinion. Moreover, the university as an institution has developed in modern times into a much different reality than it was, even a little over a century ago when Cardinal Newman wrote his "Idea of a University." That classic book can no longer be a complete model for the Catholic university of today. Also, one should reflect that Cardinal Newman never realized even in his day what he wrote about so well.

The *pax britannica* and the colonies have given way to the newly independent and largely frustrated third world. The mainly rural world of the nineteenth century has now become largely urbanized. The population explosion has almost tripled world population in the last hundred years or so. Vatican I has been followed by Vatican II. We have progressively passed through two world wars and a whole series of brush wars, some unhappily still in prog-

---

[1] Philip Hughes, *A Popular History of the Catholic Church* (New York, 1954), pp. 225–226.

ress. We have experienced an industrial, communications, nuclear and space revolution. Ecumenism is supplanting many of the ancient and bitter religious and cultural rivalries. Never before has there been so much discussion and action about human rights and human development.

It is not surprising that universities have reflected increasingly in their structure and programs all of these revolutionary developments. Nowhere has this been more striking than in America. We inherited Newman's Idea of the British University as an exclusively teaching institution, added on the concept of graduate and research functions from the German university model, and, to further complicate the institution, have elaborated since the end of World War II a new university function of service to mankind on the local, state, national and international levels.

Apart from tripling the goals, the internal structure of the American university has undergone considerable change as well. Freedom and autonomy are still central to the university's life and spirit here and everywhere, but here they are buttressed by a system of governance that involves diverse layers of power and decision: Boards of Trustees, faculty, administration, alumni and students. All are not equal members of this uneasy balance of power, but each group can and does have its say. Sir Eric Ashby has remarked in a recent book that the whole system is very complicated and very imperfect, but somehow it has worked and we have yet to find a better one.

Theodore M. Hesburgh, C.S.C.

This then, in the briefest kind of shorthand, is the world into which the Catholic university is being reborn. One must remember that the Church did not create this modern university world, as it helped create the mediaeval university world. Moreover, the Church does not have to be present in this modern world of the university, but if it is to enter, the reality and the terms of this world are well established and must be observed. The terms may be complicated and unlike operating terms within the Church itself. The reality of the university world may make the Church uneasy at times, but all university people throughout the world recognize this reality and these terms as essential to anything that wishes to merit the name of university in the modern context. One may add descriptive adjectives to this or that university, calling it public or private, Catholic or Protestant, British or American, but the university must first and foremost be a university, or the qualifiers qualify something, but not a university.

I should add frankly at this time that many people in the university world and outside it take a dim view of the very possibility of a Catholic university. George Bernard Shaw put it most bluntly when he declared that a Catholic university is a contradiction in terms. I presume that he viewed the Church of his day as an essentially closed society and the university as an essentially open society. This is a considerable oversimplification with which I shall deal later, given the developments of Vatican Council II. The

The Vision of a Great Catholic University

core of the answer to Shaw must, of course, be that a university does not cease to be free because it is Catholic. Otherwise, I am not sure an answer is possible. A recent magazine article (PACE, January, 1968) carries on its cover a title: "Notre Dame, Can it be both free and Catholic?" And an article in *Harper's* magazine was entitled: "Notre Dame, The First Great Catholic University?"

A more recent critic of any Christian institution of higher learning is Dr. Harvey Cox. In his *Secular City*, he says that "The idea of developing Christian universities in America was bankrupt before it began." Later on in the same Chapter 10 he asks, "What is the role of the Church in the university?" And he then answers his question: "The organizational Church has no role. It should stay out." I have taken up Professor Cox's argument at some length in an address to the Council of Protestant Universities and Colleges last January in Los Angeles. Suffice it for now to say that, if the Churches had stayed out of higher education from the founding of Harvard in 1636 until the Morrell Act of 1863, there would have been precious little higher education in this country, including no Harvard where Dr. Cox is now teaching. This is hardly bankruptcy in any normal sense of the word. I realize that Dr. Cox is speaking throughout the chapter to the actual situation of today. Even here though, I have tried to demonstrate in the talk mentioned above that what can be done by Christians in a secular university can be done equally as well, if not better, in a Christian university. I would make this case strongly for his first two tasks of reconciliation and criticism. I am less confident regarding his third task of creative disaffiliation, mainly because I am not convinced that this is as important as Dr. Cox makes it, as a mandate for Christian action in the world he describes. Anyway, Dr. Cox does add a certain unwelcome attitude to the task we are undertaking: to create a great Catholic university in the world today. This is, perhaps, the understatement of the year.

This negative atmosphere is also found within the Catholic Church. Dr. Rosemary Lauer, formerly of St. John's University, declared on the occasion of a debacle there that the Church should get out of education, indicating that the results to date were questionable. Another more reasoned doubt came from my good friend, Miss Jacqueline Grennan, as she secularized her formerly Catholic Webster College. I do not question her action, a valid experiment in our times, but we should consider her statements: "The very nature of higher education is opposed to juridical control by the Church"; and "The academic freedom which must characterize a college or university would provide continuing embarrassment for the Church if her hierarchy were forced into endorsing or negating the action of the college or university."

In answering this objection, one sees the clear value of the initiative that Notre Dame took last year in placing the University under a new form of governance, a Board of Trustees completely compa-

The Vision of a Great Catholic University

rable to any other university Board, with more than four times as many lay as clerical members. Under this new form of governance, fully approved by the Holy See, the University of Notre Dame is a civil, nonprofit, educational corporation, chartered by and operating under the civil law of the State of Indiana, totally directed by this largely lay Board of Trustees. To describe this as "juridic control by the Church" would be simply untrue. Our University might more properly be called a secular institution, but I would prefer not to thus characterize it, because of the contemporary implications of secularism and secularization which would not apply in a professedly Catholic university.

While this institution is not under the "juridic control of the Church" in the sense used by Miss Grennan, a small minority of us here, as priests or religious, are by our own choice under certain juridic control by the Church, not precisely as to our university functions, but as to our personal lives as priests and religious. The Catholic laity here, in their personal lives, are also loyal to the teachings of the Church as they freely choose to be members of the Church. Their faith is their business just as someone else's lack of it is his. It seems helpful to remember here a wonderful text from Vatican II's *Church in the World Today:* "In order that such persons may fulfill their proper function, let it be recognized that all the faithful, clerical and lay, possess a lawful freedom of inquiry, and [freedom of] thought and the freedom to express their minds humbly and courageously about those matters in which they enjoy competence."[2]

As to the academic freedom that Miss Grennan mentions, our official University statement in our Faculty Manual is in full accord with that of all other universities in the land. In actual performance, I cannot recall a single breech of this freedom in the twenty-two years I have taught and administered here. One of our Jewish professors, when asked recently by a reporter if he found the University free, said, "The freedom here is frightening."

On Miss Grennan's final point of the embarrassment of the Church or the hierarchy in being forced to endorse or negate the actions of a Catholic university, I simply say there is no such pressure on the Church or the hierarchy under Notre Dame's present form of governance which places it as an institution under civil, not canon law. The University is not the Church. It might be said to be *of* the Church as it serves both the Church and the people of God, but it certainly is not the magisterium. It is not the Church teaching, but a place, the only place, in which Catholics and others, on the highest level of intellectual inquiry, seek out the relevance of the Christian message to all of the problems and opportunities that face modern man and his complex world.

I would be the last to claim that this Catholic uni-

---

[2] Walter M. Abbott, S.J., ed., *The Documents of Vatican II* (New York, 1966c), p. 270.

The Vision of a Great Catholic University

versity, or some other, will not at times be an embarrassment to the Church or the hierarchy because of the actions of some faculty member, administrator, student or a group of these. Universities have no monopoly on the misuse of freedom, but few institutions on earth need the climate of freedom to the extent that universities do, whatever the risk involved. Moreover, it should be said that universities since their founding in the Middle Ages have always been unruly places, almost by nature, since the university is the place where young people come of age, an often unruly process; places where the really important problems are freely discussed with all manner of solutions proposed, places where all the burning issues of the day are ventilated, even with hurricane winds at times. Again, by nature, the university has always been dedicated uniquely to criticism of itself and everything else, even, or perhaps especially, in the case of the Catholic university, those things held most dear.

The university is not the kind of place that one can or should try to rule by authority external to the university. The best and only traditional authority in the university is intellectual competence: this is the coin of the realm. This includes, in the Catholic university especially, philosophical and theological competence. It was great wisdom in the mediaeval Church to have university theologians judged solely by their theological peers in the university.

There will always be times when embarrassment might seem to be avoided by attempting to silence someone of unusual views or eccentric personality. Church and State share this temptation equally, with the Church coming off better today, I believe. In most cases where this temptation is indulged, only greater embarrassment ultimately comes, especially to the cause of the university, the higher learning, the Church and the State. As Cardinal Newman said so well: "Great minds need elbow room, not indeed in the domain of faith, but of thought. And so indeed do lesser minds and all minds."[3]

By now, it should be clear why we need the pioneering virtues mentioned above to attempt to create what to many seems impossible, a great Catholic university in our times. The time has come to define more positively just what we have in mind, no matter how difficult a task this is. I addressed myself to such a statement earlier this year in writing an introduction to our new Faculty Manual. I shall now draw on that statement and add to it.

A great Catholic university must begin by being a great university that is also Catholic. What makes a great university in the ancient and modern tradition that we have been discussing? First and foremost, it must be a community of scholars, young and old, teaching and learning together, and together committed to the service of mankind in our times. It might be hoped that in a university worthy of the name the young learn from the old and vice versa, that the faculty grows wiser as it confronts

[3] *Idea of a University*, 4th Ed. (London, 1875), p. 475.

The Vision of a Great Catholic University

the questioning, idealism, and generosity of each new generation of students, and that the students draw wisdom and perspective from their elders in the academic community. Any university should be a place where all the relevant questions are asked and where answers are elaborated in an atmosphere of freedom and responsible inquiry, where the young learn the great power of ideas and ideals, where the values of justice and charity, truth and beauty, are both taught and exemplified by the faculty, and where both faculty and students together are seized by a deep compassion for the anguishes of mankind in our day and committed to proffer a helping hand, wherever possible, in every aspect of man's material, intellectual and cultural development. I believe that John Masefield, poet laureate of England, had all of this in mind when he wrote that the university is a splendid place. A great university must be splendidly all of this, or it is neither a university nor great. And let us candidly admit that many so-called universities today are neither.

Now the great Catholic university must be all of this and something more. If we at Notre Dame, today and tomorrow, can be all of this and something more, then the bottom drops out of the objections we have been considering. What is the something more? Here we can indeed take a page from Newman's book, where he says eloquently that there must be universality of knowledge within the university. Catholic means universal and the university, as

Catholic, must be universal in a double sense: first, it must emphasize the centrality of philosophy, and especially, theology among its intellectual concerns, not just as window dressing, not just to fill a large gap in the total fabric of knowledge as represented in most modern university curricula. Rather theology in the Catholic university must be engaged on the highest level of intellectual inquiry so that it may be in living dialogue with all the other disciplines in the university. Both philosophy and theology are concerned with the ultimate questions, both bear uniquely on the nature and destiny of man, and all human intellectual questions, if pursued far enough, reveal their philosophical and theological dimension of meaning and relevance. The university, as Catholic, must continue and deepen this dimension of intellectual discourse that was badly interrupted, to our loss, several centuries ago.

The second sense in which the Catholic university must be universal is related to the first, perhaps a corollary of its philosophical and theological concern. Without a deep concern for philosophy and theology, there is always the danger that the intellectual and moral aspects of all human knowledge become detached and separate. Technique can become central, rather than the human person, for whom technique is presumably a service. Social scientists can close their eyes to human values; physical scientists can be unconcerned with the use of the power they create. Stating all of this is not to say that all other knowledges in the Catholic university are ruled by a philosophical or theological imperialism. Each discipline has its own autonomy of method and its proper field of knowledge. The presence of philosophy and theology simply completes the total field of inquiry, raises additional and ultimate questions, moves every scholar to look beyond his immediate field of vision to the total landscape of God and man and the universe. One might turn the words of Shaw around and say that no university is truly a university unless it is catholic, or universal in this sense.

Now may I bring all of this back to Notre Dame and our goals as we look ahead today. Some may worry a bit about what has just been said if it is phrased in terms of a commitment of this University as Catholic. I submit to you that we have overdone our fears about this word "commitment," which has become a kind of dirty word in university circles. Universities which exclude philosophy and theology as an integral part of the university education have also made a commitment. Some scholars are committed to agnosticism, atheism, scientism, humanism and a whole host of other positions. Is our commitment less sacred or less permissible in the university world? Certainly not, if we make our commitment freely and intelligently. Should those who live peacefully with a host of alien commitments be denied their own? Should a commitment to wholeness and universality of knowledge by whatever means in an institution that calls itself a university be looked upon as retrogressive? I make no apology for any of my free commitments. I can live and work in the total academic community with all who profess other commitments. I only ask that it not be done in the name of uncommitment, which it is not, and that our intellectual respect for each other be mutual.

At Notre Dame, as in all universities, commitment to be meaningful must be personal rather than institutional, a thing of personal free conviction rather than institutional rhetoric. I think we have been able to do this at Notre Dame in a large ecumenical fashion. Whatever the personal faith of our variegated faculty and student body, I have sensed that we are united in believing that intellectual virtues and moral values are important to life and to this institution. I take it that our total community commitment is to wisdom, which is something more than knowledge and much akin to goodness and beauty when it radiates throughout a human person.

If all of this is largely true, then I think that Notre Dame can perform a vital function in the whole wide spectrum of American higher learning, doing what many other institutions cannot or will not do. We can, in summary, give living vital witness to the wholeness of truth from all sources, both human and divine, while recognizing the inner sacredness of all truth from whatever source, and the validity and autonomy of all paths to truth. Somehow, the Notre Dame community should reflect profoundly, and with unashamed commitment, its belief in the existence of God and in God's total revelation to man, especially the Christian message; the deep age-

The Vision of a Great Catholic University

long mystery of Salvation in history; the inner, inalienable dignity and rights of every individual human person, recognizing at the same time both man's God-given freedom and his human fallibility, an uneasy balance without God's grace; buttressing man's every move towards a more profound perception and articulation of truth and a more humane achievement of justice in our times—and Notre Dame must try to do all of this in the most ecumenical and open spirit. Somehow, all of this Judeo-Christian tradition should be reflected here at Notre Dame in the very humane atmosphere of this beautiful campus, in a spirit of civility as well as of love, in openness as well as in commitment, in our humble pilgrim search as well as in our enduring faith and hope. We may do all of this poorly, but we cannot, if we aspire to be a great Catholic university in the modern context, attempt to do less.

What kind of a place will Notre Dame be in the years ahead if all of this happens here? First, I think it will bring to light, in modern focus, the wonderfully traditional and ancient adage: *intellectus quaerens fidem et fides quaerens intellectum.* How to say it for today? Let me begin by saying that modern man stands or cowers beneath a mushroom cloud. He has created it and in a sense it symbolizes all his efforts of self-destruction across all the ages. Yet he seeks a deeper meaning. Life cannot be simply negation and despair, so he seeks a faith: in God, in God's Word, in God Incarnate, in Christ Our Lord, in suffering and resurrection, in life eternal. These are the only realities that keep man today from the ultimate despair. Thus is the faith that man seeks in this place, faith as a gift, faith that sets the mind of man to soaring beyond the limits of human intelligence, on the level of divine intelligence, into the realm of the beyond.

A modern novelist, Morris West, has put this thought in words that speak to man today: "The believers are the lucky ones. They make a mockery of the death sentence. . . . But belief is a gift, like poetry or divination or the wonderful imagination of a happy child. . . . The believer, who says: 'I believe this or that, and my belief gives me all the answers I need for survival.' But whatever the standpoint, to arrive there involves an act of acceptance. Without this act of acceptance, sanity is impossible: There is only the howling confusion of a wasteland. . . . It is not difficult for me to believe in the existence of God. For me the word 'God' is three letters in the Roman alphabet that signify an Unknown and an Unknowable who is the active origin of the universe. I do not see, feel or hear Him. My act of faith in His existence is a daily leap through a paper hoop. I think the leap is no less reasonable—and for me it is more reasonable—than the act of the man who stands and does not leap. I do not condemn him. . . . Some kind of gift—in the Christian vocabulary it is called "grace"—is always needed to make a projection from the known into the unknown. . . . Because we have suffered together, we are patient with each other. We have learned that

The Vision of a Great Catholic University

we do not walk with equal steps; that while one is strong, the other stumbles; that when one is blind, the other must lend his eyes; and that when we both come to the frontiers of faith, one may be given the gift, while it is withheld from the other. But the bond of love is still unbroken, and this is what still unites the man who has jumped through the paper hoop and the man who has not yet made the leap. . . . We are men and women, granted the same gift of existence upon this spinning earth, condemned to the same suffering and the same death, given equally the promise that none of us will be left orphans."[4]

Intellectus quaerens fidem—the mind of man reaching out for a faith—this is one side of the coin. The other is *fides quaerens intellectum:* faith seeking in the university community an expression of belief that will be relevant to the uneasy mind of modern man. This means in a word that we cannot be satisfied here with mediaeval answers to modern questions. We cannot, for example, speak of war as if the bow and arrow had not been superseded by the nuclear intercontinental ballistic missile. Faith is unchangeable in what it believes, but as good Pope John said, there are many ways of expressing what we believe—and today, the words must be directed to the inner complexity of our times, as Manzoni said, in *I Promessi Sposi,* "Guazzabuglio del cuore umano": The utter confusion in the heart of man.

---

[4] M. West, "Testimony of a 20th Century Catholic," *America,* December 2, 1967, 678–688.

Theodore M. Hesburgh, C.S.C.

The university is best prepared to understand this human confusion, and to speak to it with faithful words that say something, to avoid the meaningless formulae, the empty phrases, the words without weight. If the Catholic university can fulfill this first function of the human mind seeking faith, and faith reaching out for an expression adequate to our times, it will indeed be a great light in the all encompassing darkness that engulfs our world today. Such a university will be faithful to the wisdom of the past, relevant to the present, and open to the future.

Secondly, the Catholic university must be a bridge across all the chasms that separate modern men from each other: the generational gap of the young and old, the rich and the poor, the black and the white, the believer and the unbeliever, the potent and the weak, the East and the West, the material and the spiritual, the scientist and the humanist, the developed and the less developed, and all the rest. To be such a mediator, the Catholic university, as universal, must have a foot and an interest in both worlds, to understand each, to encompass each in its total community and to build a bridge of understanding and love. Here the name of the game is peace, not conflict. Only in such a university community can the opposite sides discuss matters civilly and not shout at each other. Only in such a university community can there be the rational and civil discourse that builds bridges rather than widens the gulfs of misunderstanding. If this cannot be done here, then the human situation is hopeless,

The Vision of a Great Catholic University

and we must resign ourselves to hatred, noise, violence, rancor and ultimately the destruction of all we hold dear.

Thirdly, the Catholic university must be a place where all the intellectual and moral currents of our times meet and are thoughtfully considered. How great is the need today for a place where dialogue is civil, not strident, where all ideas are welcome even if not espoused, where hospitality reigns for all who sincerely have something to say. Where else, except in the Catholic university, can the Church confront the challenges, the anguishes, and the opportunities of our times? Where else can there be an *agora* such as that in which St. Paul spoke of the unknown God in Athens?

Schema Thirteen of Vatican II addressed many problems of the Church in the world today. This document is an invitation rather than an ultimate answer. If the ultimate answers are to be found, these must be found within the Catholic university community which is in living contact with the faith and the world, the problems and all the possible solutions, the possibilities and the despairs of modern man. In the modern Catholic university every sincere and thoughtful man should be welcome, listened to and respected by a serious consideration of what he has to say about his belief or unbelief, his certainty or uncertainty. Here should be the home of the inquiring mind, and whatever the differences of religion, culture, race or nationality, here should be the place where love and civility govern the conversation, the interest and the outcome. Jacques Barzun called the university the House of the Intellect. The Catholic university should, beyond all else, be this house, as well as the house of civility and lively discussion in the cause of truth which unites us all in its quest and in its promise.

Let us now return to where we began: to the possibility of a great Catholic university in our times, since this is the ultimate challenge to Notre Dame on this occasion. I would like to describe one more dimension to the vision proposed above. Here, my guide is Father Teilhard de Chardin, a modern prophet despite the problems that attend his vision. Father Teilhard envisioned two parallel paths of human development: one natural that involved the humanization of all creation by man, another supernatural that would Christianize the total world. The natural goal was Omega, the supernatural was called Pleroma, or the recapitulation of all things in Christ, Our Saviour. Teilhard believed that man would naturally give himself to the process of humanizing the world as we know it. This process would be attended by all manner of human frustration and despair, especially when all of the ambiguities and human negations bear upon man. For Teilhard, there was only one guarantee of human perseverance in the quest of natural progress: the parallel path of salvation history, of the grace of God in Christ, the deep belief that ultimately the Omega and the Pleroma would merge in the new creation. Otherwise, despite his deep belief in the

The Vision of a Great Catholic University

upward and the onward, Teilhard knew nothing but despair.

I think we can find in this Teilhardian presentation an analogy or a prototype for the Catholic university. All universities are committed to human development and human progress in the natural order of events. This whole endeavor is ultimately a fragile thing, left to itself, fraught frequently with frustration and often despair. Here in the total spectrum, the Catholic university does have something spectacular to offer. Call it faith, call it belief, call it a simple parallel course depending on other sources of strength, other sources of knowledge, a belief in an ultimate goal surpassing all natural endeavor. The Catholic university must be all that a university requires and something more. It may be that the Teilhardian parallel is the something more, the extra element that defies frustration and despair. However you measure it, we here on this occasion commit ourselves to the something more, not in a spirit of being superior, but with the humble realization that we must be ourselves at Notre Dame, in keeping with our tradition, and that, hopefully, being ourselves will mean that we may add something to the total strength of what we most cherish: the great endeavor of the higher learning in our beloved America and in our total world. How more splendidly can we be a splendid place?

SERMON

Delivered by His Excellency,
The Most Reverend
Luigi Raimondi Apostolic Delegate

TODAY'S LITURGY SINGS THE PRAISES OF MARY IMmaculate and applies to her words that Scripture attributes to Wisdom in the work of creation. Wisdom is personified and is associated with God in shaping the universe, in the wondrous process of the formation of earth, sea and sky, and impressing on them the mark of splendor and beauty.

The creative process is repeated, as it were, in God's marvelous plan of salvation. Our Lady, as the chosen Mother of Wisdom Incarnate, was present from all eternity in the mind of God and is inseparably associated with her Son in his salvific mission. It is thus that the sublime language of Wisdom is applied to Our Lady. Mary was to become the exalted model of the church and, therefore, she can rightfully say to all men: "Happy those who keep my ways. Happy the man watching daily at my gates, waiting at my doorposts. For he who finds me finds life, and wins favor from the Lord." (Prov. 8:34–35)

This feast of Our Lady provides a most appropriate setting for the commemoration of a milestone in the history of this institution. In fact the University of Notre Dame was born, has developed and flourished under her auspices. Throughout its entire life it has been linked to Our Lady with a golden thread of devotion and love. Her lighted statue stands on this campus as a symbol of its ideals and she has dominated events at this great center of studies and culture, always active in the heart and mind of the members of the University. To the heavenly Queen, whose name is so proudly borne by this University, and who is at the heart of this celebration, we offer today the expression of our fervent devotion and gratitude for her maternal protection.

On this memorable occasion we cannot but recall the unlimited confidence placed in Our Lady by Father Sorin, the founder of this University, who most appropriately could have said: "When this School, Our Lady's school, shall grow more, I shall raise her aloft so that all men shall know why we succeeded here. To that lovely Lady, raised high on the dome, a golden dome, men may look and find the answer."[1]

The celebration of the one hundred and twenty-

---

[1] Arthur J. Hope, C.S.C., *Notre Dame, One Hundred Years* (Notre Dame, Indiana, 1948), p. 64.

Sermon

fifth anniversary of Notre Dame offers us an opportunity to assess both its academic and scientific achievements and its contributions to the religious and spiritual life of the country. This University has truly become an outstanding example of Catholic thought and culture. Since its humble beginnings to the impressive reality of today, there has been a wonderful succession of struggles and achievements that mark the history of this renowned institution. It all started on the day when Father Sorin conceived the plan of raising, near a log cabin and a wooden chapel, a four-story building in honor of Our Lady. In it the children of the early settlers of this remote and undeveloped land were to receive an education. Only two years later it was officially recognised as a university under the title of Notre Dame-du-Lac, Notre Dame of the Lake. The small seed was confided in faith and love to a generous soil. Because it had in itself the secret of life, it has gradually grown into the splendid reality which we witness today.

In their missionary zeal, Father Sorin and his companions were led by the desire to mold new generations of well-educated Christians, since they were convinced that no amount of secular learning is enough if it is not matched by a proper religious and moral training. It was an ideal to which they gladly consecrated their entire lives. Generations have passed by, times have changed, but the spirit, proudly called the spirit of Notre Dame, and the ideals have remained.

The Second Vatican Council has reaffirmed the

right and duty of the Church to educate her children as being related to the divinely conferred mandate to preach the mystery of salvation to all men and to restore all things in Christ. Although concerned primarily with man's spiritual and supernatural destiny, the Church is aware of the intimate connection between that destiny and the whole of man's life, for even the earthly part of it has a bearing on his heavenly calling.[2]

In the mind of the Church, education must be directed to the development of all man's faculties and to the fulfillment of all his legitimate aspirations in view of his final destiny. Education should help to promote "that Christian transformation of the world by which natural values, viewed in the full perspective of humanity as redeemed by Christ, may contribute to the good of society as a whole."[3]

These principles are in themselves sufficient to justify Catholic education at all levels. It is our conviction that Catholic education on the college and university level is more needed today in this rapidly developing world than at any time in the past. The era of Catholic universities is far from being over. Their role, which is closely associated with the role of the Church in the world, appears particularly valid in relation to problems such as the concept of

---

[2] "Declaration on Christian Education," *The Documents of Vatican II,* ed. Walter M. Abbott, S.J. (New York, 1966ᶜ), pp. 636–639.

[3] Ibid., p. 640.

Sermon

God, the new humanistic trends, and the progressive unification of mankind.

The present crisis of faith, the tendency to secularization, the stress on subjective conscience and personal values as against the natural and divine positive laws, is a result of a loss of the proper concept of God's transcendence. This holds true also in regard to the notions of creation, the supernatural order of redemption and grace, and the ultimate meaning of human history. The impact that these basic concepts have on education and culture is evident.

Problems of this nature did not escape the attention of the Conciliar Fathers, who restated the existence of a double order of knowledge, namely, faith and reason. The two orders are distinct but not contradictory; rather, they are complementary to one another. Faith refers to God's revelation of Himself, the destiny of man, his redemption and the plan of salvation. Far from being the result of a blind and irrational impulse, faith is the conscious, free response of man to God's call to salvation. It cannot be acquired by human means nor can it be the result of a mere process of reasoning. It is a gift from God, Who wills to grant it to every person, but it requires the willing acceptance and conscious cooperation of the individual. The deposit of revealed truth has been entrusted by Jesus Christ, the Son of God, to his Church, which has thus become the depositary, custodian and herald of the divine message to be communicated to all men through her infallible magisterium by those who, with and under Peter, through apostolic succession, receive the mandate and charisma of teaching, sanctifying and governing the Church.

A question often asked today is whether faith is still relevant to the mind of the modern man. With this in view, the Second Vatican Council on the closing day directed to men of thought and science a special message in which we read: "Why a special greeting for you? Because all of us here, bishops and Fathers of the Council, are on the lookout for truth. . . . Hence our paths could not fail to cross. Your road is ours. Your paths are never foreign to ours. . . . Never perhaps, thank God, has been so clear a possibility as today for a deep understanding between real science and real faith, mutual servants of one another in the one truth. . . . Have confidence in faith, this great friend of intelligence. Enlighten yourselves with its light in order to take hold of truth, the whole truth."[4]

In its Pastoral Constitution on the Church in the Modern World, the Council warned about the danger of relying solely on reason . . . ". . . Today's progress in science and technology can foster a certain exclusive emphasis on observable data, and an agnosticism about everything else. . . . The methods of investigation which these sciences use can be wrongly considered as the supreme rule for discover-

---

[4] "Closing Messages of the Council," *Documents,* pp. 730–731.

Sermon

ing the whole truth . . . however, these sciences cannot penetrate to the intimate meaning of things."[5] Truly, the danger exists that man, confiding excessively in modern discoveries, could reach the conclusion that he is self-sufficient and has no need to seek higher realities. While admitting the achievements of the physical and natural science, faith adds a new dimension to human existence. It teaches man that he has been made partaker of divine nature and a sharer in an eternal inheritance. In the words of a famous modern thinker: "Science, alone, cannot discover Christ, but Christ fulfills the aspirations that are born in our hearts at the school of science."[6]

In our time, great emphasis is placed on humanism as an ideal and a basis for relations among men. Man is conceived of as the center on which everything else must converge, for he is seen as the measure of all things. He is thus inclined to be intolerant of anything that might interfere with his own personality. Yet at the same time a growing process of depersonalization and dehumanization is evident. The role of men in society appears often difficult to define. The individual man is often absorbed in an anonymous mass incapable of defending and asserting himself.

The humanism that the Church offers not only recognizes and respects the dignity of the human person, but lends it a character of sanctity and gives

[5] *Documents,* p. 263.
[6] Teilhard de Chardin, *Science et Christ,* (Paris, n.d.), p. 62.

it a more solid foundation. It makes man more conscious of his responsibilities as a member of the community. An example of such humanism is to be found in the Encyclicals *Mater et Magistra* and *Pacem in Terris* of Pope John XXIII and *Populorum Progressio* of the reigning Pope Paul VI. It was to this form of humanism that Pope Pius XII referred when he said: "The Church takes to herself the fullness of all that is human, wherever and however she finds it, and transforms it into a source of supernatural energy."[7]

Although divided by ideological, political, and religious barriers, mankind strives for greater unity. No one can question that today a more universal form of culture is being developed which promotes and expresses the unity of the human race. To that aim tend the manifold activities and exchanges among nations directed to the strengthening of the social, ethnic and cultural bonds of their peoples.

The Church can and is anxious to play a vital role in the process of the unification of mankind. Her doctrine, her emphasis on brotherhood and love, on equality and respect for the God-given rights of the human person, cannot but foster that unity among peoples which is one of their deeply felt aspirations. Thus the Council Fathers proclaim: "By her relationship with Christ, the Church is a kind of sacrament or sign of intimate union with

---

[7] Vincent A. Yzermans, ed., *The Major Addresses of Pope Pius XII, Vol. II: Christmas Messages* (St. Paul, Minnesota, 1961), p. 95.

God, and of the unity of all mankind. She is also an instrument for the achievement of such union and unity."[8]

One of the primary aims of the Vatican Council was to make the Church open to a dialogue with the entire world, and to offer her services, as well as her spiritual and moral forces, for the good of all men. Evidence of this is the encouragement that the Council Fathers gave to the ecumenical movement. ". . . The Father wills that in all men we recognize Christ our brother and love him effectively in word and in deed. By thus giving witness to the truth, we will share with others the mystery of the heavenly Father's love." . . . [The Church is convinced that the] "dialogue, which can lead to truth through love, excludes no one. . . . If we have been summoned to the same destiny, which is both human and divine, we can and we should work . . . in order to build up the world in genuine peace."[9]

As members of the Church in constant touch with the trends of the human spirit and its yearnings, we must become ever more conscious of our duty as bearers and witnesses of a message of truth and love, in which all men are called to share. This is particularly the task of an institution worthy of the name "Catholic." Adaptation to the needs and the historical context of our time must go hand in hand with a continuous effort to renew oneself spiritually,

[8] "Dogmatic Constitution on the Church," *Documents,* p. 15.
[9] "Pastoral Constitution on the Church in the Modern World," *Documents,* pp. 306–307.

through fidelity to the spirit of the gospel and the principal requirements of a Christian life.

It is in the light of these thoughts and considerations that we envisage the future of this University. Today's celebration is more than a mere tribute to its founders and to those who have helped its growth and expansion. It is also a testimony to the ideals that have characterized and sustained the University for the past one hundred and twenty-five years. It is proof of the determination of its present directors to face the future with the same intention and the same faith in the conviction that Christian principles will help to dispel confusion in men's minds and guide them to brighter horizons, mindful of what the Psalmist tells us: "The Truth of the Lord remains forever" (Ps. 116:2).

We are fully confident that Notre Dame, proud of its past achievements and conscious of its role as a Church institution in the field of culture and the sciences, will strive along this path with the youthful vigor that it has always had. We have no doubt that in fidelity to the spirit, which has made it respected and renowned, this University will be able to transmit with dignity and honor the Christian message of faith, optimism and hope to generations yet to come. This is our sincere wish today. For this we offer our fervent prayers to Our Lady, the Seat of Wisdom, the sweet and powerful Protectress of the University of Notre Dame.

REMARKS

The following was an after-dinner speech delivered by Mr. Edmund Stephan, Chairman of the Board of Trustees, at the One Hundred and Twenty-Fifth Anniversary luncheon on December 9, 1967. It is reported here in all its charming informality as part of the official documentation of the celebration.

Your Excellencies, Reverend Fathers, Reverend Brothers, Reverend Sisters, distinguished guests, ladies and gentlemen:

I am honored to be with you today and to be able to thank you on behalf of the Board of Trustees and the whole Notre Dame family for joining us in this commemoration of the one hundred twenty-fifth Anniversary of the founding of the University.

We have a custom here at Notre Dame of not making lengthy speeches at luncheons and as illustrious and moving as this occasion is I do not think an exception should be made today. I am sure you will all be grateful for this fidelity to tradition—there's so little of it left anymore.

This is my first day at this convocation. After hearing the kind of talk we had presented this morning by Dr. DuBridge, I regret that I could not be here from the beginning.

Perhaps I am repeating sentiments already expressed—but I think this is an appropriate moment to pay high tribute to the priests of the Holy Cross Order who in the past century and a quarter have carved this wonder of a great modern university out of what was once a bleak Indiana wilderness. It is difficult to imagine how any group of men could have lived more productive lives and done so much for all those who follow. Through Father Craddick, representing Father Kenna, the Provincial of the Order who could not be with us today, may we send our felicitations and gratitude to all members of the Order.

I must now single out one person for a special word. Notre Dame has been blessed with a long line of distinguished Presidents but I don't believe any one has brought more inspiration, talent and dedication to this office than Father Ted Hesburgh who has carried the burdens of the presidency for the past fifteen years—and burdens they are—but always with good humor and deep compassion for those around him.

Father Ted, there are other universities which have much greater endowment funds than Notre Dame, but I wouldn't trade you for a $100 million addition to ours. Anything beyond that figure I might have to take up with the Board—but I would do so reluctantly.

Incidentally, one of the nice things about having a Board of Trustees is that it can make fitting re-

Remarks

marks about the administration which it cannot make about itself.

I wish there were time to mention how we feel about Father Joyce and the many others who perform so brilliantly here but I must adhere to the tradition of brevity I have mentioned.

I have referred to the Board of Trustees and it of course has been a well publicized fact that about six or seven months ago the governance of this University passed from clerical to lay control in a real legal and effective sense. This change, new in the life of Catholic institutions, reflects many of the new attitudes in our society and the reexamination of policies and procedures that is taking place within the Church itself. I feel that it is terribly important not only for Notre Dame but for church-affiliated institutions generally that this experiment succeed and that it play a vital part in bringing this University to new and higher levels of achievement. The Trustees, I can say, pledge themselves to this task.

Our new Board assumes its duties at a difficult juncture in the history of private education in this land. There is the life-and-death struggle for financial survival which I would guess will always be with us; there is the unending search for talent in faculty and administration and even on Boards of Trustees. There is the growing dependence on government funds, necessary and beneficial in many ways but bringing with it a special set of problems —though I must say I gained a new insight into this subject this morning from Dr. DuBridge. And then there is, of course, the perplexing matter of student unrest—many use stronger words—expressing itself in so many ways that are odd and troublesome to people of my generation. On this latter point I take some comfort from the thought that restlessness and ferment are a natural condition of the university milieu and should not unduly disturb us. I do not know anyone who pretends to understand fully what lies beneath the so-called revolt of the younger generation, but I would suggest that if any place is equipped to deal with it, it is the university, with its tradition of civility, its respect for the human spirit and its appeal to reason and virtue over passion and discord.

On the subject of discord. In academic life, as in so many other aspects of human existence, there can be no genuine freedom without order; yet we must recognize, too, the converse proposition, that in the academic community, of all places, one would not have much order without freedom. In fact, one would not have an academic community at all. Anyone who would sacrifice one for the other will surely end up having neither.

The first imperative for any institution is to preserve its essential character. This, it seems to me, involves the drawing of some lines, and I might say holding them, with respect to the activities of those who live and function within it. Tolerant lines, understanding lines, lines that should not be drawn at all in case of serious doubt, especially in an academic environment, but some boundaries beyond which abuse of the institution and everyone else in it cannot be permitted.

Freedom and order are always in delicate balance in any venture involving human beings. To strike the right balance in the academic community seems to me to be one of the issues looming large in our day—one calling for great wisdom and surely for great patience. I have been going on too long. I will close by expressing great hope for the future of this institution and abundant thanks to all who have brought it to where it is today.

Thank you very much.

SEGRETERIA DI STATO
DI SVA SANTITÁ

N. 107810

DAL VATICANO, November 21, 1967

Very Reverend and dear Father,

It is by special personal mandate of the Sovereign Pontiff that I convey to you His cordial salutation and prayerful good wishes on the occasion of the hundred and twenty-fifth anniversary of the founding of the University of Notre Dame.

On the great feast of the Immaculate Conception of Our Lady, Patron of the United States of America, His Excellency the Apostolic Delegate will celebrate a solemn Mass to mark this completion of a century and a quarter of outstanding service to Catholic higher education. Present in spirit at the Divine Sacrifice, and mindful of His particular union with the University as its Doctor "honoris causa", the Holy Father prays that Notre Dame may ever be an ardent beacon of faith and truth, upholding the highest university principles and traditions, "having confidence in faith, this great friend of intelligence", and enlightening all "with its light in order to take hold of truth, the whole truth" (Message of the Second Vatican Council to Men of Thought and Science).

May the Sovereign Master of all thought, Who entrusted to us the mysterious lamp which is faith, Who alone said and could have said: I am the Light of the world, I am the way, the truth, and the life (cf. ibid.) bestow His richest graces of guidance and illumination upon the University of Notre Dame. With this prayer, His Holiness cordially imparts to you, Father President, to the faculty, staff and students, and to all who unite with you in observing its anniversary, His special paternal Apostolic Benediction.

With my personal felicitations and good wishes, I remain

Sincerely yours in Christ,

A. G. Card. Cicognani

The Very Reverend Theodore M. Hesburgh, C.S.C.
President
The University of Notre Dame

NOTRE DAME, Indiana 46556

THE WHITE HOUSE

WASHINGTON

December 5, 1967

The University of Notre Dame began on a ten-acre clearing in the Indiana wilderness one hundred and twenty-five years ago. It became one of the great universities of the world. Its history reflects the history of our country -- to which the sons of Notre Dame have made outstanding contributions. You have grown with the country -- and you have helped make your country great.

This convocation is an appropriate moment for your President to express to the men of Notre Dame, past and present, the gratitude of a nation enriched by their individual excellence and their common dedication to public service.

I am confident that, so long as our nation endures, Notre Dame will continue to add luster to herself -- and distinction to our country.

Lyndon B. Johnson